A TRIBUTE TO HULL'S FISHING INDUSTRY

Compiled by

Michael Thompson

From photographs

by Donald Innes

HUTTON PRESS
1996

Published by

The Hutton Press Ltd.,
130 Canada Drive, Cherry Burton,
Beverley, East Yorkshire, HU17 7SB.

Printed and bound by
Clifford Ward (Bridlington) Ltd.,
55 West Street, Bridlington,
East Yorkshire, YO15 3DZ

ISBN 1 872167 86 1

CONTENTS

FOREWORD

Donald commenced his lifelong interest in photography by forming his own business "Graphic Pictures" shortly after the end of the Second World War. He named his company after the legendary 5x4 press camera, the Speed Graphic, which was used by leading press photographers throughout the world. The cameras were heavy and unwieldy to use from the moving deck of Charles Ayres' boat, often in poor weather conditions. As well as carrying the camera there was the even heavier leather case full of double dark slides containing the glass plates onto which the valuable images were recorded. Great care had to be taken that you did not slip on the deck or fall into the Humber, or worst still drop the valuable camera into the murky depths. A hip flask and a supply of cigarettes completed the essential equipment to combat the cold foggy mornings.

Photography of moving trawlers was no easy matter. One of the most important shots was the broadside. This had to be taken when you could see through the centre of the winch forward of the bridge whilst running at full speed. You only had one chance and if you missed it you would have to chase several miles down the Humber, as Charlie's boat was somewhat slower than the powerful trawler engines.

The notoriously thick Humber fogs were also quite perilous and seemed to coincide with photography sessions. On many occasions we simply had no idea where we were, or where our trawler had disappeared to.

Fishing trip shots were taken by another member of the Innes team, Les Samson, who had joined the studios after service in the Royal Navy. Sam was sent away for a three week trip, and as well as taking photographs he was expected to assist with the crew's duties whilst at sea.

My own memories are of my father wrapped in his familiar belted heavy overcoat and trilby, both of which he seemed to wear at all times; the endless wait for Charles Ayre's boat at the lockpit on cold winter mornings; the searing pain in the end of your finger tips as you waited for your fingers to warm, up until they were warm enough to operate the camera (using gloves was an impossibility). In spite of all this, he was able to contribute to the unique collection of photographs for our enjoyment some 50 years later.

Ivor Innes
Hessle 1996

Donald Innes

4

INTRODUCTION

During 1948 Donald Innes was commissioned by the shipbuilders Cook, Welton & Gemmell to photograph the launch ceremony of new vessels at the company's Grovehill shipyard on the banks of the River Hull at Beverley. And also to photograph the completed vessels as they ran their proving "trials" on the River Humber.

Whilst out on the River Humber in Charlie Ayre's boat Donald Innes also took the opportunity to photograph trawlers as they passed by on the way to St. Andrew's Dock or outward bound to the fishing grounds.

From the 1950's Donald Innes was employed by the British Transport Docks Board to photograph new developments and improvements to the Hull Docks system. A large amount of this work was centred on St. Andrew's Dock.

It is now 20 years since St. Andrew's Dock closed and the combination of these two contracts have left us with a superb set of images of the once great fishing industry. A selection of these has been chosen to illustrate this book.

Michael Thompson
July 1996

ACKNOWLEDGEMENTS

The author gratefully thanks:

Niki Innes for typing the manuscript.
Steve Betts for producing the photographs.
Craig Kirby for drawing the Fish Dock map.
Arthur G. Credland for reading and checking the historic data.
Finally his wife, Margaret, for her patience and support.

Front cover:

Bottom left — A deckhand joins his trawler the *Northella* H159 circa 1951, with his kitbag over his shoulder and a new pair of thigh boots from the dock's stores. He is dressed in the traditional trawlerman's suit with wide bottom trousers.

Top rght — Outward bound from St. Andrew's Dock on the high tide during 1955 is the trawler *Stella Polaris* H575.

Bottom right — On the Iceland market in the 1950's filleters are at work "cutting" fish. Alongside them is the trawler *Kingston Diamond* H243.

CHAPTER 1
CHRONOLOGICAL HISTORY OF HULL'S FISHING INDUSTRY

1160

A deed known as the Camin Charter, granted a fishery in the River Humber to the monks of Meaux Abbey.

1517

Hull City records show that a fish shambles was established in Fish Street. At this time the port of Hull had important trade links with Iceland and Scandinavia, one of the main imports being salt fish.

1840's

The "Silver Pits", rich fishing grounds were discovered not far from the mouth of the River Humber.

Brixham and Ramsgate sailing smack owners began to make a temporary base at Hull, whilst engaged in the summer fishery off the Yorkshire Coast, taking advantage of the influx of summer visitors to Scarborough. Some of the smacks' owners brought their catches to Hull which with a population of 67,000 was a good outlet for fish sales.

1840

The completion of the Hull and Selby Railway in 1840 provided the first rail link to the growing population of the North and Midlands for the transportation of the much needed supply of fresh fish.

1850

Encouraged by the success of the local North Sea fishery a number of Brixham smack owners settled at Hull.

1854

30 sailing smacks were registered at the Port of Hull.

1855

The Fishing Fleet had grown to almost 100 vessels. As mooring space became limited the fishermen were considered a source of inconvenience to the Hull Docks Company.

1850's

The Boxing Fleet system was introduced. Each day the smacks' catches were rowed across to a fast cutter which took the fleet's catch to Billingsgate fish market in London. When the smacks returned to Hull for stores they landed their catch at the Hull market.

1859

Fjord ice was imported from Norway for use in the fishing industry.

1864

A decision was taken to replace the sailing cutters with 4 steam carriers. Two the *Lord Alfred Paget* and *Wellesley* were introduced in 1865. and 2 more the *Hallet* and *Frost* in 1866. These carriers could carry 3,900 boxes of fish packed in the hold between layers of crushed ice. Over 270 smacks were now registered at Hull.

1869

The opening in 1869 of the West Dock, later named Albert Dock, gave the fishing fleet a new home and the opportunity for the coherent development of the fishing industry.

1876

One of the earliest fleets was the "Red Cross" fleet owned by the Hull steam Fishing and Ice Company, which was founded in 1876. In 1880 the company ordered 4 steam carriers from Earle's Shipbuilding Yard, Hull. The steam carriers took the catches to Hull as well as London. They were named *Africa, America, Asia* and *Europe*.

1880

The Great Northern Steam Ship Fishing Company was founded. The company built its first fish carrier in 1882, named *Eastward*. By 1880 the Hull fleet had grown to some 400 vessels.

1883

The "Great Storm" raged through the North Sea during 6th March 1883, when 47 smacks sank with the loss of 260 men. 27 of the smacks were Hull vessels making it the port's worst day for disasters.

1883

Hull's St. Andrew's Dock opened on Monday 24th September 1883. At the time of opening the Hull Fishing Fleet numbered about 420 smacks of 70-85 ft in length. The dock was named after the patron Saint of fishermen.

1885

Hull's first steam trawler the *Magneta* H1447 joined the fleet, built by Cook, Welton and Gemmell at Hull for F. & T. Ross. She was 95 feet long and 52 net tons.

1886

Two more steam trawlers the *Lark* and the *Linnet* joined the Hull Fleet.

1887

Although a number of sailing smacks were built for a few more years, from a peak in 1887 of 448 smacks they gradually began to decline.

1888

Hellyer Brothers Ltd. were founded, also The "Gamecock" Fleet of Kelsall Brothers & Beeching Ltd. which began to operate out of Hull in 1894.

1880's

By the late 1880's the North Sea was already seeing the effects of over fishing. Vessels began to fish further out from the North Sea grounds. Some returned to the historic fishing grounds of Iceland during the summer months. This included both sailing and steam powered vessels.

1890

From 1890 increasing numbers of Hull and Grimsby steam trawlers began to fish the rich Iceland grounds. Unfortunately the British fishermen adopted a cavalier attitude towards the local Icelandic fishermen ruining their livelihood. Eventually the Danish Government had to send a gunboat to police the area.

The Hull Fish Meal and Oil Company was founded and a factory built to handle the large amount of fish offal from the market. The waste products were turned into fish meal. Fish landed at Hull in 1890 totalled 19,839 tons.

1891

The first ice manufacturing factory was established by the Hull Ice Company. The plant was capable of producing 50 tons of ice per day.

1893

On 1 July 1893 the Hull Docks Company was bought out by the North Eastern Railway Company and the Hull Docks were added to the North Eastern Railway system.

1894

During a series of storms in the North Sea in December 1894, 6 Hull steam trawlers and 9 Hull smacks were lost and 106 men lost their lives. The worst day was 22 December when 9 Hull vessels sank.

1897

The Hull Fishermen's Widows and Orphans Fund was set up on 11 May 1897, for relief in cases of distress of the widows, children and dependants of the 106 men lost in December 1894. Both trawler owners and fishermen paid contributions to the fund.

The St. Andrew's Dock extension was opened. At the extreme western end a slipway was built where trawlers could be hauled out of the water for surveys and repairs.

1899

The "Salt Fish" industry began at Hull in 1899. Large quantities of cod were split, salted and laid out on racks in the open to be dried by the wind, in an area to the west of the dock known as the "cod farm".

In 1899, 2 Hull steam trawlers were wrecked at Iceland, the first of many such casualties in this area.

1900

With the introduction of even larger trawlers Hull fishermen began to explore the distant Arctic grounds off Norway and the Barents Sea, although the North Sea remained the single most important source of fish caught by Hull trawlers.

In 1900 fish landed at Hull totalled 62,900 tons.

1903

The last of the sailing smacks was sold out of the Hull fleet. All the port's trawlers were steam powered.

1904

The Dogger Bank Incident (Russian Outrage). During the early morning half light of 22 October 1904, the Hull "Gamecock" fishing fleet of some 40 vessels was trawling near the Dogger Bank. It was encountered by the Russian Baltic Fleet which was en route to the Far East where the Tsar was engaged in a war with Japan. The Russian Navy officers mistook the Hull trawlers for Japanese torpedo boats and opened fire on them for 20 minutes. The trawlers were bombarded with almost 300 shells. During the attack 2 fishermen were killed and 7 injured, and the trawler *Crane* was sunk.

Protests were made to the Russian Government who paid compensation amounting to £65,000. The Russian Baltic Fleet steamed on to its destruction at Tsu-Shima in May 1905.

1906

On the 30 August 1906 a memorial was unveiled to the victims of the Russian Outrage. It was erected outside St. Barnabas Church on the corner of Hessle Road and the Boulevard where it still stands.

1907

Admiral Lord Charles Beresford, while visiting East Coast fishing ports, recommended in the event of war that steam trawlers should be used for minesweeping duties to free warships for other duties. In 1907 fish landed at Hull totalled 79,664 tons.

1911

Along with the white fish trade, Hull became the kippering centre of Britain with some 50 smoke houses for haddock and herring, 89% of the produce being exported. In 1911 half of the wet fish coming into Hull (42,377 tons) was herring from Scandinavia, brought to Hull by cargo vessels.

1913

Successful experiments with Marconi Marine radio sets on Hellyer Brothers' trawlers *Othello* and *Caesar* led to the wide use of the equipment by the 1920's. Fish landed was 80,382 tons which was sold for £989,456. A high price was paid in ships and men with 11 Hull trawlers lost in 1913.

The Hull fleet had grown to 389 vessels, 259 fleeters and 130 single boating vessels.

1914-18

In 1914 with the outbreak of the Great War the Admiralty requisitioned many trawlers for minesweeping duties. Almost 800 trawlers entered war service from the Hull and Grimsby fishing fleets.

The North Sea grounds were closed due to the danger of enemy action and fleeting was suspended for the duration. By 1915 only a quarter of the pre-war Hull fleet remained in fishing. Most of these were transferred to the West Coast port of Fleetwood.

During the war over 200 British trawlers were lost. 62 Hull trawlers were lost whilst in service with the Royal Navy.

The first motor lorry to work on the fish dock was registered on 14 March 1917, owned by Allenby Bros., the Harrow Street carriers.

1919

After the Great War the fishing industry went through a decade of great change. At sea the distant water grounds began to take preference over the North Sea. During 1919 the Great Northern Steam Ship Fishing Company and the Hellyer Brothers' boxing fleets ceased fleeting and went into single boating operations.

In 1919 the Hull fleet numbered 226 vessels, 139 single boating vessels and 85 fleeting vessels. Fish landed totalled 58,991 tons worth £2,445,175.

1920's

Until the 1920's fish was dispatched from the Hull market whole or headless. Then the fillet was introduced as a more convenient method of distributing fish. This break-through not only reduced carrying costs by half, but also created a large new labour force of filleters and packers. Charles W. Jordan is reputed to have been the first merchant to fillet fish on the Hull market. Fish landed in 1920 was 97,788 tons, value £2,670,162.

1921

The "Gamecock" fleet of Kelsall Brothers & Beeching Ltd.

and "Red Cross" fleet of the Hull Steam Fishing & Ice Company Ltd. merged to form a fleet of 80 boxing fleet vessels.

1922-1928

The 1920's were a time of great prosperity for the fishing industry. Between 1922-28 86 large distant water trawlers were built for Hull trawler owners.

1923

From 1 January 1923, the ownership of the Hull docks passed to the London and North Eastern Railway Company.

1924-1929

For a period of 5 years Hellyer Brothers operated part of their trawler fleet from Hafnarfjordur in Iceland. Also they owned a number of trawlers which were registered at Iceland with Icelandic names, but carried Hellyer's livery.

1925

In 1925 Hellyer Brothers bought two refrigerated cargo ships and converted them to Portuguese type dory mother ships for "long lining" for halibut, named *Arctic Queen* and *Arctic Prince*. The ships unloaded their catch of frozen halibut in Albert Dock which was close to St. Andrew's Dock. In 1935 the ships were laid up, then sold to the U.S.S.R. and became part of the Russian Government fleet.

1927

The first trawler owner to fit radio-telephone to their vessels was Pickering and Haldane's Steam Trawling Company, with equipment by Marconi Marine. Three years later the first Marconi Echo meter was made available to fishermen. This equipment was very successful as it was not only a navigational aid, but was also used to locate shoals of fish.

1928

By 1928 200 British trawlers were equipped with wireless.

1929

In 1927 work began on modernising the Hull fish markets. During 1929 when the work was almost complete, a large fire destroyed the No. 2 market.

The fire which was discovered at 7.15 pm on Sunday 15 August 1929 became so great that although the entire Hull City fire brigade was soon at the scene their main task was to prevent the fire from spreading.

The landing stage with over 100 merchants' offices was destroyed, along with 105 railway wagons. Seven trawlers were badly damaged. 3, *Ohm Lord Deremore* and *Marconi*, were burned out.

1930

The Hull fishing fleet numbered 301 vessels, 229 single boats and 72 in the boxing fleet. Fish landed totalled 209,531 tons which sold for £2,550,808.

1931

During the 1930's the Hull trawler owners embarked on a big expansion programme, which resulted in over fishing. The market became depressed and large amounts of unsold fish were sent along with the offal to the fish meal factory. For example on Whit Monday 1931, 6,000 ten-stone kits of good quality cod were sent to the fish meal factory because even at the low asking price of 6 shillings a kit they could not be sold. The Hull Fish Meal Factory was the biggest in the world, with a daily intake capacity of 1,000 tons.

1932

In 1932 to try to elevate the depressed state of the market, there was a voluntary withdrawal from the Barents Sea and Bear Island grounds between August and September.

1934

Until 1932 fish livers were kept in barrels and brought back to Hull to be processed by the Hull Fish Meal & Oil Company. The crews were paid so much "liver money" per barrel.

About 1930 experiments took place in boiling livers at sea, which produced a high quality oil which was developed into the fine product it is today.

In 1934 the Hull trawler owners bought out the assets of the oil department of the Hull Fish Meal & Oil Company and set up their own company British Cod Liver Oil Producers (Hull) Ltd. In 1935 a new factory at Marfleet began to produce the finest cod liver oil in the world.

1935

Between 1930-39 the Hull fishing industry suffered a large number of tragic trawler losses. A total of 30 trawlers were lost or wrecked, 11 with all hands. One of the most poignant of the losses was that of the *Edgar Wallace*, which hit a sand bank and capsized abreast of the fish dock, on 9 January 1935 with the loss of 15 of her 18 crewmen. Having just endured a winter fishing trip she was lost in sight of home.

In March 1935 at a time when trawler owners and crews were earning very little money due to low fish prices, the owners decided to reduce the "liver oil" money by 10 shillings a barrel. This brought the whole fleet out on strike. The local community supported the trawlermen with a strike fund, into which money was paid each week by pubs, shops and members of the public. The dispute lasted 3 weeks during which some 246 trawlers were tied up at the Hull Dock. The trawler owners realising the crews had nothing to lose by being at home relented and the fleet returned to sea.

1936

During March 1936 Kelsall Bros. and Beeching and the Hull Steam Fishing & Ice Company went into liquidation and the boxing fleet was laid up for sale. Declining North Sea catches and high fuel costs had made the operation uneconomical. Approximately 500 fishermen and a large number of shore workers lost their jobs.

Between May-October 1936 an embargo of Barents Sea and Bear Island grounds came into effect, which was to last until 1939.

1937

By 1937 the rapid expansion of the fishing industry brought its own problems. Despite the demise of the boxing fleet, 1937 yielded a record catch of 328,447 tons. The market collapsed and prices fell to rock bottom. Fortunately the trawler owners recognised the problem and an "economic investigation" research unit was established in an office on St. Andrew's Dock. This undoubtedly saved the industry. Prices were rationalised and uneconomic trawlers were laid up, sold or scrapped. Fish landings, which peaked in 1937, were reduced to 196,400 tons in 1939.

1930's

During the 1930's when the Hull fish market had its heaviest ever landings, an average of 350 fish vans (each with a capacity of 4 tons) would leave the dock in 8 special express freight trains. In their heyday these trains served 1,000 stations and 4,000 distribution points.

1939-45

In September 1939 with the outbreak of the Second World War, the Admiralty began to requisition trawlers for use as minesweepers and anti-submarine patrol vessels. Out of the Hull fishing fleet of around 277 vessels, some 260 trawlers were taken into naval service along with their crews. During the war 70 Hull trawlers were lost whilst serving with the Royal Navy. Also 8 were lost whilst carrying out their normal fishing work.

With just a few old trawlers left to fish in restricted areas the Hull fishing industry had to rely on a fish carrier service from Iceland to supply a small amount of fish. In 1941 only 2,607 tons were landed, 1942 — 6,316 tons, 1943 — 13,877 tons and 1944 —18,648 tons. By the end of 1945 landings had grown to 49,326 tons.

With the dock virtually closed down most of the work force went into the armed forces.

During an air raid on 15 March 1941 a parachute mine fell in St. Andrew's Dock. When the mine was detonated on 18 March by Naval Authorities the explosion caused extensive damage to the No. 1 market. In another raid Pickering and Haldane's office and the eastern end of the dock were badly damaged.

From 1944 the Admiralty began to release a few of the older trawlers from the Navy to be converted back to their fishing role. Also the Government allowed trawler owners to place orders with shipyards for new trawlers when peace returned.

1945

As the war in Europe drew to a close, the Admiralty released most of the remaining requisitioned trawlers from the navy and ship repair yards throughout Britain were given the work of converting the vessels back to their fishing role. And when they were de-mobbed the fish dock workers returned to their former jobs.

At Hull the fleet was placed under the temporary management of the Hull Ice Company, the reason for this being that all the Hull trawler owners were shareholders in the concern and would receive a share of the profits until such time as normal fleets could be built up.

1946

By 1946 the shipyards had begun delivering new vessels , among which were the first oil fuel burning trawlers the *St. John* and the *Southella*, also the experimental motor trawlers *Allan Water* and *Thorina*.

When the deep water trawlers returned to the North East Arctic grounds which had been closed for 6 years, they found enormous shoals of fish. Consequently trawlers began landing record catches onto a previously starved market.

But as a result of the increased catches the price of fish fell and in June 1946 the crews of Hull and Grimsby trawlers went on strike against low prices. A court of enquiry was set up to investigate the dispute, which resulted in a National Joint Council being formed to deal with such disputes.

Fish landed in 1946 was 373,216 tons from a fleet of 136 trawlers.

1947

On 7 March 1947 there was another strike when Hull trawler crews demanded the abolition of the dual duties of the deckhand, who also had to trim coal in the engine room. By 19 March, 76 trawlers were laid up, but a week later an agreement was reached through the N.J.C. where vessels over 160 feet could carry an additional permanent trimmer.

1948

On 1 January 1948, all the nation's railways, road, transport, docks and waterways were nationalised and the ownership of St. Andrew's dock passed to the British Transport Commission.

1949

Delivered in January 1949, the Hull trawler *Benella* owned by J. Marr & Son Ltd. was the first such vessel to be fitted with radar. Eventually the whole fleet was fitted with at least one set, often two.

During 1949 the last coal burners were built for Hull trawler owners. The Lord Line was the last major Hull company to order coal burners, taking delivery of: *Lord Rowallan* (Jan 1949), *Lord Willoughby* (Feb 1949), *Lord Cunningham* (May 1949) and *Lord Fraser* (May 1949), from Cochrane's of Selby. Also delivered in May 1949 was *Cayton Bay* for the Marine Steam Fishing Company, from Cook, Welton and Gemmell of Beverley. All these vessels were later converted to burn fuel oil.

1940's

Post-war Hull trawler losses in the 1940's were *Loch Hope* which trawled a mine at Iceland on 11 June 1947. One crewman was lost and 8 injured. *St. Amandus* was wrecked at Norway on 24 December 1947, but all her crew were saved. The Hull based *Sargon* was wrecked at Iceland on 1 December 1948 whilst making for shelter in a blizzard. A group of rescue workers from the Icelandic Coastguard Service managed to save 6 crew from the *Sargon*, but 11 men perished. The *Spaniard* was wrecked at Norway on 23 March 1949. All her crew were saved.

1950

By 1950 another depression had hit the fishing industry. Fish merchants were struggling to make a profit and trawlers were barely covering their running costs.

In February 1950 Hull trawler engineers and firemen went on strike over their share of "liver oil" money which was an important part of the trawlermen's pay when fish prices were low. At the peak of the strike 130 vessels were laid up. After 17 days an agreement was reached and the men returned to sea from the 4 March.

In August 1950 the Hull Fishing Vessel Owners Association decided to lay up 20% of the fleet. This once again involved the older uneconomic vessels. The lay-up of vessels during summer months lasted until September 1954.

In 1950, 217,655 tons of fish were landed with a value of £7,786,752 from a fleet of 160 trawlers.

1951

During 1951 the White Fish Authority was set up by Parliament to reorganise, develop and regulate the British white fish industry with responsibility for the whole industry from catcher to retailer to consumer.

From 1947 trawler owners had begun converting vessels from coal burners to fuel oil. The main considerations for this were running costs and improved efficiency. From 1951 the predominance of the coal burners went into decline. Out of a fleet of 165 vessels 80 were coal fired and 85 oil fired.

1950-1953

During the early 1950's Hull trawlers resumed fishing at Greenland, an unpopular area because of poor navigation charts and severe weather. In 1951 Hull trawlers began to exploit a new fishing ground south of Cape Farewell, 300 miles nearer home than the traditional north coast grounds.

On 4 November 1952, the Hull trawler *Norman* was wrecked at South Greenland in thick fog. 20 of her crew were lost, one man was saved.

Then in 1953, 4 Hull trawlers which were "salting" at Greenland narrowly escaped being lost in severe weather, just reaching Godthab before capsizing from the build up of ice.

1952

On 15 May 1952 the Icelandic Government declared a 4 mile fishing limit measured from the headlands. This cut off 5,000 square miles of first class grounds which Iceland claimed were being overfished and excluded her own vessels as well. This led to a ban on Iceland trawlers landing at all British ports, imposed by the British fishing industry.

On 12 May 1952, the new Queen Mary hostel of the Royal National Mission to Deep Sea Fishermen was opened in Goulton Street.

1953

Efforts by the London millionaire George Dawson to bring Icelandic fish to the Humber ports met with strong opposition and the scheme fell through.

On 2 June the coronation of Her Majesty Queen Elizabeth II was celebrated with street parties and other events. The Hull trawler *Loch Doon* represented the Hull fishing fleet at the Spithead review on the 15 June.

By the end of 1953 Hull's 20 trawler owners declared an aggregate loss of £590,000 for the year.

1954

The Silver Cod Challenge Trophy was introduced in 1954. The "Silver Cod" was awarded by the British Trawler Federation to the skipper and the crew of the trawler with the largest total catch of the year. The first winners in 1954 were the crew of the *Arctic Warrior*.

1955

On 26 January 1955 the Hull trawlers *Lorella* and *Roderigo* were lost in severe weather off Iceland with the loss of all 40 crewmen. The whole city of Hull went into mourning.

From the mid 1950's the price of fish gradually increased and the outlook for the industry improved. It was estimated that some 50,000 local people were employed in work associated with the fishing industry. Of these 3,400 were trawler crew and 640 were registered bobbers.

1956

During 1956 after lengthy negotiations a compromise was reached between Britain and Iceland over the disputed 4 mile limit.

On 4 April a 100 yard section of the No. 1 Quay caved in, the subsidence being the result of wartime land mine damage. On 28 September a further 50 yard section of dock wall collapsed. In the previous December the docks board had announced plans to spend £170,000 on a new scheme to replace the damaged section of the No. 1 Quay.

Post-war fish landings peaked in 1956 at 258,944 tons valued at £12,482,445.

The first diesel-electric trawler for the Hull fleet, *Portia*, was built at Middlesbrough for Hellyers.

1957

On 17 January 1957 the Icelandic trawler *Isolfur* became the first Icelandic vessel to land at St. Andrew's Dock for over 4 years.

Over the years many prominent visitors to the City of Hull expressed an interest in visiting the "fish dock". In May 1957, St. Andrew's Dock was spruced up for a visit by Her Majesty the Queen and His Royal Highness Prince Philip. This visit gave the local workforce a rare opportunity to see the royal couple at close hand.

1958

Built during 1958 at Beverley for the Newington Steam Trawling Company, the *Joseph Conrad* was the last steam trawler built for the Hull fleet.

On 23 June 1958 the Icelandic Government declared a 12 mile fishing limit from 1 September 1958. This was to lead to the first of the acrimonious disputes between Britain and Iceland known as the Cod Wars.

British trawlers fishing between the 4-12 mile limit did so in "boxes" under the protection of the Royal Navy Fishery Protection Squadron.

During the "Cod Wars" the amount of fish caught by Hull trawlers remained consistent despite harassment from Icelandic gunboats.

1959

In 1946 Icelandic fishing interests donated £20,000 to Hull City

Council for housing relief, following the devastation of the 1939-45 War. In 1959 Hull Corporation completed 9 bungalows and 18 flats for elderly seafarers and their dependants. The estate was named Icelandic Close.

On 28 August 1959 the *Staxton Wyke* was lost 9 miles off Hornsea, following a collision with the Newcastle ore-carrier *Dalhara*. Five of the trawler crew were lost. The *Staxton Wyke* was one of 11 Hull trawlers lost in the 1950's.

1960

In 1960 the Hull fishing industry entered the era of the large combines. In February Ross Group of Grimsby, who already owned Charleson-Smith Trawlers, took over Hudson Brothers Trawlers, giving Ross Group a combined fleet of 22 trawlers.

Ross Group also tried to take over Kingston Steam Trawler Company and Loch Fishing Company. But Hellyer Bros. held off the take-over bid and managed to acquire the controlling interest in Kingston and Loch for themselves.

In 1961 Hellyers (39 trawlers) merged with Associated Fisheries whose Lord Line fleet consisted of 21 trawlers, a total of 60 trawlers.

Boyd Line Ltd. (12 trawlers) and T. Hamling & Company (11 trawlers) formed a joint management to operate their 2 fleets from one office.

So by 1961, 3 major groups controlled 105 of the Hull fleet of 141 distant-water trawlers.

This left only 4 other owners, J. Marr & Son Ltd., St. Andrew Steam Fishing Company, Newington Trawlers Ltd., and Henriksen & Co.

1961

On 28 February 1961, Britain accepted the 12 mile Iceland fishing limit. In March 1961 Norway also extented their limit to 12 miles. British trawlers were given conditional concessions to fish up to 6 miles off the coastlines.

On 30 June 1961 the *Lord Nelson*, Hull's first stern fishing trawler, arrived from the German ship building yard, Rickmers Werft, Bremerhaven.

1962

On 11 July 1962 the *Junella*, Britain's first wholefish freezer stern trawler, arrived at Hull.

1962 saw the end of Hull's coal-burning trawler fleet when in August the last 3 coal-burners were laid up. The *Othello* had the distinction of being the last to do a trip. The other 2 were *Kingston Ruby* and *Loch Oskaig*. All 3 were scrapped in Belgium in 1963.

1963

In February 1963 a new canteen was opened for the use of all fish dock workers. The canteen provided hot meals and snacks for up to 18 hours a day. Housed in St. Andrew's Dock Chambers the canteen was paid for by the Hull Fish Merchants Association.

In March 1963 the Beverley shipyard of Cook, Welton and Gemmell was faced with closure. The yard was taken over by the local engineering firm C. D. Holmes.

Built in 1963 by Cochranes at Selby for Ross Group (Hull), the *Stella Altair* (Sept.) and *Stella Sirius* (July), were the last side fishing trawlers built for the Hull fleet.

1964/65

In July 1964 British Railways under the Beeching re-organisation announced their plans to reduce the number of Hull fish trains from 8 to 2 a day.

From 1 February 1965 Hull fish train services were reduced to 1 a day, the 6.35 pm London Kings Cross. When later in the year this service was also withdrawn the local carting agents and road transport companies happily took over the role of distributing the whole of Hull's inland fish.

1965

In June 1965 work on a new 340 foot section of No. 1 quay for the unloading of freezer steam trawlers was completed.

On 22 November 1965 Ross Group decided to re-name the trawlers of the Hull subsidiaries Hudson Bros. (*Cape's*) and Charleson-Smith (*Stella's*) with the Ross prefix; also the fleets adopted Ross funnel colours.

In February 1966 all vessels in the Associated Group's Hull fleet were re-registered under the name of Hellyer Bros. Ltd. The trawlers were painted in Hellyer colours and so the well-known companies, Loch Fishing Co. Ltd., Northern Fishing Co. (Hull) Ltd., Kingston Steam Trawling Co. Ltd., Lord Line Ltd. and West Dock Steam Fishing Co. Ltd., completely disappeared from the scene.

1966

On 16 November 1966 the freezer trawler *St. Finbarr* left Hull for the coast of Labrador. On Christmas Day 1966 a disastrous fire swept through the trawler claiming the lives of 12 crewmen. The Hull trawler *Orsino* rescued the 13 survivors and took the stricken *St. Finbarr* in tow, but she sank on 27 December.

It is worth noting that 40 ships of various nationalities responded to come to the aid of the *St. Finbarr*.

1967

During 1967 there was industrial unrest involving the bobbers, ship repair workers and Hellyers shore gang. Also an Industrial

Court rejected the British Fishermen's pay claims.

Hull's first factory trawler *Coriolanus*, owned by Hellyer Bros. Ltd., arrived at the port on 12 May 1967. By the end of the year 13 freezer stern trawlers were sailing from Hull.

1968

The most far reaching event in 1968 was the tragic loss of 58 men and 3 trawlers during the opening weeks of the year. The *St. Romanus* disappeared on passage to the Norwegian Coast about 11 January during bad weather. Then between 26-27 January the *Kingston Peridot* was lost off North Iceland followed by *Ross Cleveland* lost on 4 February whilst sheltering in Isafjordur. Only one crewman survived. Public outcry over trawler safety led to a 10,000 signature petition being taken to the House of Commons to be handed to Prime Minister Harold Wilson.

An independent committee of inquiry into trawler safety was set up under the chairmanship of Admiral Sir Derek Holland-Martin. This led to the *Orsino* being chartered as a "mother ship" to assist British trawlers fishing at Iceland during the winter months.

1969

Following the events of 1968 and pressure from the trawlermen's union, the Silver Cod Trophy discontinued. The last winner was the skipper and crew of the *Primella*.

On 27 March 1969 the *James Barrie* was wrecked in the Pentland Firth. Fortunately on this occasion all the crew were saved. The *James Barrie* was one of 9 Hull trawlers lost during the 1960's.

On 1 July 1969 Associated Fisheries merged with Ross Group to form British United Trawlers. The Company took over a fleet of 120 trawlers under the management of a number of subsidiary companies of most of Britain's fishing ports.

By the end of 1969 Hull's fleet of 93 trawlers consisted of 22 freezers and 71 wet fish trawlers. Oil burners had declined from 115 in 1960 to 40 vessels in 1969, the majority being motor driven.

1970

In March 1970 bobbers set up a new port record when they landed 331 tons of frozen fish from the *Arctic Raider* in an 8 hour shift.

Due to the large number of freezer trawlers using the port it was decided to extend the freezer berth by another 340 feet.

1972/3

On 1 September 1972 the Icelandic Government unilaterally declared a 50 mile fishing limit, a move rejected by the European fishing nations. Once again the British Fleet had to fish in "boxes" under the protection of the Royal Navy.

In October 1973 the new limit was officially recognised. Access within the new zone was strictly limited, and close season and conservation areas were established.

During 1972 talks were held between the British Transport Docks Board, the trawler owners and the Fish Merchants Association, to discuss a move for the fishing industry to Albert Dock. This was due to large sums of money being needed to be spent on repairs and the proposed South Orbital ring road which was to be routed close to St. Andrew's Dock.

1974

On February 8, 1974 the freezer stern trawler *Gaul* capsized and sank during bad weather conditions off the North Cape of Norway with the loss of her 36 crew.

1975

In October 1975, the Icelandic Government inflicted a major blow on the fishing industry by unilaterally declaring a 200 mile fishing limit. This provoked a year of hostility during which the British fleet continued to operate in the disputed zone. As well as the Royal Navy, civilian ships were chartered to hinder the Icelandic gunboats' attempts to cut the trawl warps of the trawlers.

Despite every diplomatic effort it proved impossible to reach a compromise, and on 1 December 1976, the 200 mile limit was recognised, and British trawlers were barred from the Icelandic grounds.

1975

In October 1975 the Hull fishing industry moved to its new base at Albert Dock. The fleet of 76 trawlers consisted of 41 "sidewinders" and 35 "freezers". At 4 am on 3 November 1975 the *Arctic Raider* was the last trawler to sail from St. Andrew's Dock.

1976

During the 1970's the price of fish greatly increased. At Hull the annual total rose from £16,246,527 for 120,589 tons in 1970, to £36,613,216 for only 62,557 tons in 1976. During 1973 the price increased by a record 45%.

Iceland was followed by Canada, Norway and Russia in establishing their own fishing restrictions in response to concern over the exploitation of the territorial waters by an increasingly large international fleet of modern sophisticated trawlers. Thus the British Deep Sea fishing fleet was now excluded from the greater part of its traditional grounds.

Another blow to the Hull fishing industry was the demise of Humber St. Andrew's Engineering Company, the trawler repair firm, where 250 jobs were lost. C. D. Holmes, engine and winch builders, and owners of Beverley Shipyard, 1963-73, also went into liquidation.

In 1976 the last 9 steam trawlers were scrapped. The *Arctic Ranger* was the last to go, arriving at Draper's, Victoria Dock slipway for scrapping on 26 October 1976.

1977

By the end of 1977 only 10 aging wet fish trawlers were still fishing. The other 16 were laid up. 17 freezers were still operating and 17 were laid up or refitting.

The number of sea-going crew on the register was 1,390. At least 200 were on the dole; landing labour was 138 men.

Due to the lack of white fish offal, the Hull Fish Meal Factory began to process large amounts of sprats and mackerel, up to 1,000 tons a week. This resulted in visiting Scottish purse seine net boats landing their catch at Hull.

1978

With the decline of the wet fish trawler fleet, the Hull Ice Manufacturing Company's factory was run down and finally closed in 1978.

In 1978 British United Trawlers transferred the last 7 Grimsby freezers to Hull. To avoid lay up of freezers, when their white fish quotas were used up, Hull trawler owners were sending their vessels to fish for mackerel in home waters.

1979/80

By the end of the 1970's the Hull fish market was increasingly dependent on foreign container imports, overland fish as well as occasional landings from foreign trawlers.

1981

By the end of 1981 only one sidefishing trawler, *Arctic Corsair*, remained at Hull. The port's once great "sidewinder" fleet had passed into the history books.

1982

During the Falklands War, Hull trawlers once again served their country when the freezers *Cordella, Farnella, Junella, Northella* and *Pict* served with the Royal Navy as minesweepers in the South Atlantic.

1983

In 1983, to help reduce the size of the British Trawler fleet, the Government introduced the decommissioning scheme of £400 per gross ton. The balance of the Hull stern trawler fleet was decommissioned and converted for survey work or sold to foreign owners. The last of the original freezer fleet to be sold was the *Pict* in 1986.

1985-86

In the mid 1980's a combination of stable oil prices, good fish prices and increasing Government support led to a new optimism in the Hull fishing industry.

Hull's last 2 trawler owners, J. Marr Ltd. and Boyd Line Ltd., made significant investment in both the local fishing fleet and new ventures in the Falkland Islands.

During 1985 the "sidewinder" *Arctic Corsair* was refitted and returned to sea. This venture proved highly successful and the trawler broke the wet fish landing record on four occasions. The *Arctic Corsair* completed her last voyage on 22 December 1987. She is now a museum ship owned by Hull City Council.

In 1986 Boyd Line acquired a factory trawler which they renamed *Arctic Ranger*. Then in 1987 the *Arctic Challenger* was returned to sea after a six year lay up. A further factory trawler was acquired in 1988 and renamed *Arctic Corsair*.

On 30 December 1986, J. Marr Ltd. placed a £5 million order with Cochranes Shipbuilders of Selby for 2 new wet fish stern trawlers. Completed in 1988 the *Thornella* and *Lancella* were the first new Hull trawlers built for over a decade. These vessels strengthened the Marr fleet of 5 ex-Fleetwood wet fish stern trawlers.

During the 1990's a further 3 modern stern trawlers have been acquired from foreign owners and added to the Marr Fleet.

1996

At the present time the Hull fish market is supplied by fish landings from the port's deep water fleet, overland fish from Bridlington and Scotland, Icelandic containers and occasional landings from Icelandic, German and Russian trawlers.

Despite all the odds, enough people from the Hull fishing industry had the resolve to fight and survive and it is thanks to these people that Hull is still a major fishing port.

CHAPTER 2
POST-WAR SHIPBUILDING AT COOK, WELTON & GEMMELL'S BEVERLEY SHIPYARD

Between 1946-1963 Cook, Welton & Gemmell built yard numbers 756 to 985 at the Beverley, Grovehill Shipyard.

These were principally trawlers for Hull, Grimsby, Fleetwood, South Africa, Belgium, Iceland and France but also tugs, coasters, minesweepers, light vessels, dredgers and barges.

From the early 1960's trawler owners began to order new larger stern-fishing trawlers and so orders for the traditional side-fishing trawlers went into decline. The last side-fishing trawlers built at Beverley for Hull trawler owners were completed in 1962.

The confined space of the river Hull at Beverley meant that Cook, Welton & Gemmell were unable to compete in the market for the large stern-trawlers and so during 1963 the yard was closed.

Various rescue plans were put forward by local concerns and in 1963 the yard was taken over by Charles D. Holmes & Company Ltd. This company, as well as building a large number of tugs also built the highly successful wetfish stern-trawlers *C. S. Forester* (1969) and the *Hammond Innes* (1972). In July 1973 ownership of the yard passed to the Drypool Group, Hull.

The trawler taking shape on the slipway is yard no. 893. To be named *Louis Trichard*, this trawler was one of an order for
three coal-fired trawlers to be built for the South African fishing company, Irvin & Johnson Ltd. Cape Town.
This view of yard no. 893 taken on the 26.5.1954 gives a good insight into the construction of a trawler. The closeness of
the frames gives the hull greater strength.

This view of the shipyard taken from the stern of a trawler being fitted out on the River Hull on 15 September 1950 shows the slipways being used to full capacity, with a further 3 trawlers in an advanced stage of construction.

Two riveters at work attaching plates to the stem of a trawler. The patchwork of plates are loosely bolted into position until all the rivets have been hammered into place. The number painted on one of the plates is 836 which was the *Kingston Jacinth*, completed in 1952.

With an almost complete hull as a backdrop a workman cuts a piece of plate to shape.
One of the many "jigsaw" pieces that will form the sturdy hull with fine lines of a Beverley designed trawler.

This photograph of carpenters at work fitting out the crew's accommodation was taken in 1950.
In older vessels fine wood panelling and brass fittings were used, but by the 1960's formica and chrome came into use.

The launch ceremony was a day of great pride, both for the owner of the new vessel and the craftsmen who had built it.

The narrow width of the River Hull at Beverley meant that vessels had to be launched sideways; this resulted in a spectacular "splash" as can be seen at the launch of yard no. 959 the *Arctic Corsair* which took place on 27 February 1960.

Vessels built at Beverley were towed down the River Hull and taken into Princes Dock, Hull where they were completed.

Moored at the premises of the engineering company Charles D. Holmes Ltd., during 1952 are the middle water trawlers *Velia*, *Idena* and *Irvana*. These were part of an order for four sister trawlers placed by J. Marr & Son Ltd., in 1950.

On 1 June 1950 the new trawler *Alamein* (H123) owned by Hull Merchants Amalgamated Trawlers Ltd. heads out of Humber Dock to run her trials on the River Humber. Once these were completed the trawler was taken to St. Andrew's Dock to take on oil fuel, stores and fishing gear and within a few days the *Alamein* would leave on her maiden voyage.

The South African coal-fired trawler *Louis Trichardt* ran her trials on the River Humber on 29 August 1954. The trawler left Hull on 1 October on the 6293 nautical mile delivery voyage to Cape Town. The *Louis Trichardt* called at Dakar for coal bunkers on 14 October and reached Cape Town on 2 November 1954.

After a successful career fishing the southern oceans the *Louis Trichardt* was taken off the fishing register on 10 February 1972. After being stripped of spare parts the trawler was scuttled off Robben Island (Cape Town). The trawler was one of a number of vessels scuttled to form a reef, which would attract crayfish to form a fishery.

st WESTHERON H465

| Gross tons: 357 | Net tons: 139 | Length 141'4" | Breadth: 24'0" |

Owner: J. C. Llewellyn Ltd., Milford Haven, managed by St. Andrew's Steam Fishing Company Ltd. Hull.
Built: 1926 by Cook Welton & Gemmell at Beverley as the *Bunsen* for F. & T. Ross Ltd. Hull. Yard No. 475
Renamed:

Jennett 1939-1946	Coal burning steam trawler Tr. Exp 3 cyl.
Westheron 1946-1950	Engine built by C. D. Holmes.
Lord Bann 1950, scrapped in 1952.	96 Nominal Horse Power. (Pre 1945 power rating for steam ships)
	Single ended boiler 200lb pressure.

st BARDIA H302

Gross tons: 375	Net Tons: 146
Length: 151'5"	Breadth: 25'0"

Owner:
Hull Merchants Amalgamated Trawlers
Ltd. Hull

Built:
1930 by Cochrane & Sons Ltd at Selby, as
the *Armana* for J. Marr & Son Ltd. Fleetwood. Yard No. 1088.

Renamed:
Bardia 1946
Scrapped in 1954.

Coal fired steam trawler Tr. exp. 3cyl.
97 Nominal horse power.
Single ended boiler 200lb pressure.
Engine built by Amos & Smith, Hull.

st VIAN H406

Gross tons: 381	Net Tons: 151
Length: 145'8"	Breadth: 25'1"

Owner:
The Ocean Steam Trawling Company Ltd.
Hull

Built:
1932 by Cook, Welton & Gemmell at
Beverley as the *Negro* for Hellyer Brothers
Ltd. Hull. Yard No. 571. Scrapped in 1957.

Renamed:
Lord Portal 1946-1948
Vian 1948.
Scrapped in 1957.

Coal fired steam trawler Tr. exp. 3cyl.
102 Nominal horse power.
Single ended boiler 200lb pressure.
Engine built by C. D. Holmes, Hull.

st HACKNESS H202

| Gross tons: 387 | Net Tons: 167 |
| Length: 151'7" | Breadth: 25'6" |

Owner:
St. Andrew's Steam Fishing Company Ltd.
Hull

Built:
1934 by Cochrane & Sons Ltd. at Selby as
the *Mendip* for W. B. Willey & Sons Ltd.
Hull. Yard No. 1128.

Renamed:
Stella Dorado 1946-1948
Hackness 1948.
Scrapped in 1959.
Coal fired steam trawler Tr. Exp. 3cyl.
106 Nominal horse power.
Single ended boiler 210lb pressure.
Engine built by C. D. Holmes, Hull.

st CARTHUSIAN H162

| Gross tons: 462 | Net Tons: 165 |
| Length: 161'8" | Breadth: 27'0" |

Owner:
Easton Fishing Company Ltd. Hull.

Built:
1936 by Smiths Dock Company Ltd.
Middlesbrough as the *Pict* for Hellyer
Brothers Ltd. Hull. Yard No. 1009.

Renamed:
Carthusian 1948
(Briefly *Stella Procyon* in 1948).
Scrapped in 1957.
Coal fired steam trawler Tr. Exp. 3cyl.
99 Nominal horse power.
Single ended boiler 225lb pressure.
Engine built by Smiths Dock Co.
Middlesbrough.

st LORD ESSENDON H312

Gross tons: 468	Net Tons: 201
Length: 161'3"	Breadth: 26'7"

Owner:
Lord Line Ltd., Hull.

Built:
1936 by Cochrane & Sons Ltd at Selby for Pickering and Haldane Steam Fishing Company Ltd. Yard no. 1158.

Scrapped in 1966.

Coal fired steam trawler Tr. Exp. 3cyl.
123 Nominal horse power.
Single ended boiler 215lb pressure.
Engine built by C. D. Holmes, Hull.

st REIGHTON WYKE H425

Gross tons: 465	Net Tons: 173
Length: 161'8"	Breadth: 27'1"

Owner:
West Dock Steam Fishing Company Ltd. Hull

Built:
1937 by Cochrane & Sons Ltd. at Selby for the West Dock Steam Fishing Company Ltd. Yard No. 1174.

Renamed:
Arctic Trapper 1959.
Scrapped in 1962.

Coal fired steam trawler Tr. Exp. 3cyl.
123 Nominal horse power.
Single ended boiler 215lb pressure.
Engine built by C. D. Holmes, Hull.

st LOCH OSKAIG H431

Gross tons: 534	Net Tons: 198
Length: 171'0"	Breadth: 28'5"

Owner:
Loch Fishing Company Ltd. Hull

Built:
1937 by Smith Dock Company, Middlesbrough for Loch Fishing Company Ltd. Hull. Yard no. 1026.

Name Unchanged:
Scrapped in 1963.

Coal fired steam trawler Tr. Exp. 3cyl.
99 Nominal horse power.
Single ended boiler 225lb pressure.
Engine built by Smiths Dock Co. Middlesbrough.

st ST. ELSTAN H484

Gross tons: 564	Net Tons: 209
Length: 172'2"	Breadth: 29'1"

Owner:
Thomas Hamling & Company Ltd. Hull.

Built:
1937 by Cook, Welton & Gemmell at Beverley for Thomas Hamling & Company Ltd., Yard no. 634.

Name Unchanged:
Scrapped in 1966.

Coal fired steam trawler Tr. Exp. 3cyl.
165 Nominal horse power.
Single ended boiler 225lb pressure.
Engine built by C. D. Holmes, Hull, converted to fuel oil July 1949 (8901 HP).

st KINGSTON DIAMOND H243

| Gross tons: 581 | Net tons: 214 | Length 178′1″ | Breadth: 30′0″ |

Owner: Kingston Steam Trawling Company Ltd. Hull.

Built: 1939 by Cook Welton & Gemmell at Beverley as *Lady Madeleine* for Jutland Amalgamated Trawlers Ltd. Hull. Yard No. 651.

Renamed:

Kingston Diamond 1946.

Scrapped in 1965.

Coal fired steam trawler Tr. Exp 3 cyl.

165 Nominal horse power.

Single ended boiler 225lb pressure.

Engine built by C. D. Holmes, Hull. Converted to fuel oil Dec. 1949 (1,000 1HP).

st BANYERS H255

Gross tons: 608	Net Tons: 207
Length: 178'1"	Breadth: 30'0"

Owner:
Henriksen & Company Ltd. Hull

Built:
1940 by Cook, Welton & Gemmell at Beverley as *St. Zeno* for Thomas Hamling & Company Ltd. Hull, but requisitioned by the Royal Navy for use as an anti-submarine trawler. Returned to Thomas Hamling in 1946. Yard no. 655.

Renamed:
Banyers 1952.
Scrapped 1966.

Coal fired steam trawler Tr. Exp. 3cyl.
165 Nominal horse power.
Single ended boiler 225lb pressure.
Engine built by C. D. Holmes, Hull, converted to fuel oil Dec, 1949 (1,000 1HP).

st COLWYN BAY H387

Gross tons: 517	Net Tons: 190
Length: 167'7"	Breadth: 28'1"

Owner:
The Marine Steam Fishing Company Ltd. Hull.

Built:
1942 by Cook, Welton & Gemmell at Beverley as H.M.T. *Duncton* (RN Hills Class) for the Admiralty. Yard no. 684.

Renamed:
Colwyn Bay 1945.
Scrapped in 1964.

Coal fired steam trawler Tr. Exp. 3cyl.
157 Nominal horse power.
Single ended boiler 220lb pressure.
Engine built by C. D. Holmes, Hull, converted to fuel oil March 1953 (890 1HP).

st CAPE GLOUCESTER H395

Gross tons: 624 Net Tons: 279
Length: 178'1" Breadth: 30'0"

Owner:
Hudson Brothers (Trawlers) Ltd. Hull.

Built:
1943 by Cook, Welton & Gemmell at Beverley as H.M.T. *Sapper* for Admiralty. Yard No. 705.

Renamed:
Cape Gloucester 1959
Admetus 1957.
Scrapped in 1966.

Coal fired steam trawler Tr. Exp. 3 cyl. 165 Nominal horse power.
Single ended boiler 225lb pressure.
Engine built by C. D. Holmes, Hull, converted to fuel oil June 1949 (850 1HP).

st STELLA CANOPUS H244

Gross tons: 579 Net Tons: 216
Length: 177'6" Breadth: 30'2"

Owner:
Charleson-Smith Trawlers Ltd. Hull.

Built:
1946 by Cochrane & Sons Ltd. at Selby as *Northella* for J. Marr & Son Ltd. Hull. Yard no. 1311.

Renamed:
Stella Canopus 1948-1965
Ross Canopus 1965.
Scrapped in 1967.

Coal fired steam trawler Tr. Exp. 3cyl. 1000 Indicated horse power.
Single ended 225lb pressure.
Engine built by Amos & Smith, Hull, converted to fuel oil Jan. 1950.

st SOUTHELLA H303

Gross tons: 534	Net tons: 192	Length 166'9"	Breadth: 27'2"

Owner: J. Marr & Son Ltd. Hull.

Built: 1946 by Cook Welton & Gemmell at Beverley for J. Marr & Son Ltd. One of the first batch of oil fired trawlers. Yard no. 768. Scrapped in 1965.

Name Unchanged: Oil fired steam trawler Tr Exp. 3 cyl. Single ended boiler 220lb pressure.
Scrapped in 1965. 1000 indicated horse power. Engine built by C. D. Holmes, Hull.

st ARCTIC HUNTER H218

Gross tons: 579	Net Tons: 216
Length: 177'6"	Breadth: 30'2"

Owner:
Boyd Line Ltd. Hull.

Built:
1946 by Cochrane & Sons Ltd. at Selby as *St. Mark*, for the St. Andrew's Steam Fishing Company Ltd. Hull. Yard no. 1310.

Renamed:
Cape Trafalgar 1947-1955.
Auburn Wyke 1955-1959.
Arctic Hunter 1959.
Scrapped in 1968.

Coal fired steam trawler Tr. Exp. 3 cyl.
1075 indicated horse power.
Single ended boiler 225lb pressure.
Engine built by C. D. Holmes, Hull, converted to fuel oil Sept 1949.

st FARADAY H195

Gross tons: 538	Net Tons: 183
Length: 169'1"	Breadth: 29'2"

Owner:
F. & T. Ross, Ltd. Hull

Built:
1947 by Cook, Welton & Gemmell at Beverley as *Nolsoyar Pall* for Chr. Holm Jacobsen Thorshaven, Faroe Islands. Yard no. 781.

Renamed:
Faraday 1951-1959.
Peter Cheyney 1959.
Scrapped in 1967.

Oil fired steam trawler Tr. Exp. 3cyl.
1000 Indicated horse power.
Single ended boiler 220lb pressure.
Engine built by C. D. Holmes, Hull.

st LORD ANCASTER H583

Gross tons: 636　　　　Net Tons: 245
Length: 177'9"　　　　Breadth: 30'8"

Owner:
Lord Line Ltd. Hull

Built:
1948 by Cochrane & Sons Ltd. at Selby for Lord Line Ltd., Hull. Yard no. 1337.

Name Unchanged:
Scrapped in 1967.

Coal fired steam trawler Tr. Exp. 3cyl. 1050 indicated horse power.
Single ended boiler 225lb pressure.
Engine built by Amos & Smith, Hull, converted to fuel oil May 1950.

st KINGSTON SARDIUS H588

Gross tons: 658　　　　Net Tons: 231
Length: 181'7"　　　　Breadth: 30'8"

Owner:
Kingston Steam Trawling Company Ltd. Hull.

Built:
1948 by Cook, Welton & Gemmell at Beverley for Kingston Steam Trawling Company Ltd. Yard no. 796.

Name Unchanged:
Scrapped in 1968.

Oil fired steam trawler Tr. Exp. 3cyl. 1000 indicated horse power.
Single ended boiler 220lb pressure.
Engine built by C. D. Holmes, Hull.

st BOSTON SEAFIRE H584

Gross tons: 689	Net tons: 249	Length 181'7"	Breadth: 30'8"

Owner: Boston Deep Sea Fisheries Ltd. Hull.
Built: 1948 by Cook, Welton & Gemmell at Beverley for Boston Deep Sea Fisheries.
Lost on the Goodwin Sands on the way to Belgian ship breakers in March 1968. Yard no. 795.

Renamed: *Cape Tarifa* 1952-1965; Oil fired steam trawler Tr Exp. 3 cyl. Single ended boiler 225lb pressure.
Ross Tarifa 1965 1075 indicated horse power. Engine built by C. D. Holmes, Hull.

st CORDELLA H572

Gross tons: 604	Net Tons: 222
Length: 170'4"	Breadth: 29'2"

Owner:
J. Marr & Son Ltd. Hull.

Built:
1948 by John Lewis Ltd. at Aberdeen for J. Marr & Son Ltd. Yard no. 202.

Name Unchanged:
Scrapped in 1965.

Oil fired steam trawler Tr. Exp. 3 cyl. 925 indicated horse power.
Single ended boiler 225lb pressure.
Engine built by J. Lewis, Aberdeen

st CAYTON BAY H72

Gross tons: 580	Net Tons: 209
Length: 171'5"	Breadth: 29'2"

Owner:
The Marine Steam Fishing Company Ltd. Hull.

Built:
1949 by Cook, Welton & Gemmell at Beverley for Marine Steam Trawling Company Ltd. Yard no. 807.

Renamed:
Bayella 1952.
Scrapped in 1967.

Coal fired steam trawler Tr. Exp. 3 cyl. 925 indicated horse power.
Single ended boiler 220lb pressure.
Engine built by C. D. Holmes, Hull, converted to fuel oil August 1955.
Last coal fired trawler built for Hull owners. Builder's model displayed in Town Docks Museum, Hull.

st BENVOLIO H22

Gross tons: 722   Net Tons: 262
Length: 184'6"   Breadth: 31'2"

Owner:
Hellyer Brothers Ltd. Hull.

Built:
1949 by Smiths Dock Co. Ltd. Middlesbrough. Launched as *Esmonde* Yard no. 1184.

Name Unchanged:
Scrapped in 1975.

Oil fired steam trawler Tr. Exp. 3 cyl.
1450 indicated horse power.
Single ended boiler 225lb pressure.
Engine built by Smiths Dock Co.
Middlesbrough.

mt LAMMERMUIR H105

Gross tons: 729 Net Tons: 265
Length: 190'7" Breadth: 32'3"

Owners:
Joint venture between Boston Deep Sea Fisheries and J. Marr & Son Ltd.

Built:
1950 by J. Lewis & Sons Ltd. Aberdeen. Yard no. 220.

Renamed:
Jegvan Elias Thomsen
(Faroes) 1956.
Scrapped in 1976.

Motor trawler oil 25A 3 cyl.
1100 brake horse power.
Engine built by Wm. Doxford, Sunderland.

35

st ST. ALCUIN H125

Gross tons: 742	Net Tons: 271
Length: 183'4"	Breadth: 30'8"

Owner:
Thomas Hamling & Co. Ltd. Hull.

Built:
1950 by Cook, Welton & Gemmell at Beverley. Yard no. 822.

Name Unchanged:
Scrapped in 1974.

Oil fired steam trawler Tr. Exp. 3 cyl.
1000 indicated horse power.
Single ended boiler 225lb pressure.
Engine built by C. D. Holmes, Hull.

st PRINCESS ELIZABETH H238

Gross tons: 514	Net Tons: 186
Length: 161'1"	Breadth: 29'2"

Owner:
St. Andrew's Steam Fishing Company Ltd. Hull.

Built:
1952 by Cochrane & Sons Ltd. at Selby. Yard no. 1380.

Renamed:
Southern Endeavour (Australia) 1959.
Sank in 1979 in the Australian 'bight'.

Motor trawler.
Oil 2S. C.SA 8 cyl.
1000 brake horse power.
Engine built by Crossley Bros. Manchester.

st LANCELLA H290

Gross tons: 790 Net Tons: 286
Length: 190'2" Breadth: 32'4"

Owner:
J. Marr & Son Ltd. Hull.

Built:
1953 by Cook, Welton & Gemmell at Beverley. Yard no. 880.

Name Unchanged:
Scrapped in 1974.
Won Silver Cod Challenge Trophy 1956 with Skipper W. Turner.

Oil fired steam trawler.
Tr. Exp. 3 cyl.
1325 indicated horse power.
Single ended boiler 225lb pressure.
Engine built by C. D. Holmes, Hull.

st CAPE COLUMBIA H118

Gross tons: 806 Net Tons: 298
Length: 188'6" Breadth: 32'10"

Owners:
Hudson Brothers Trawlers Ltd. Hull.

Built:
1956 by Cook, Welton & Gemmell, at Beverley. Yard no. 914.

Renamed:
Ross Columbia 1965-1967.
Arctic Avenger 1967.
Scrapped in 1976.
First deep water trawler built with Bulbous bow.

Oil fired steam trawler.
Tr. Exp. 3 cyl.
1400 indicated horse power.
Single ended boiler 225lb pressure.
Engine built by C. D. Holmes, Hull.

mt PORTIA H24

Gross tons: 883	Net Tons: 318
Length: 191'0"	Breadth: 34'9"

Owner:
Hellyer Brothers Ltd. Hull.

Built:
1956 by Smiths Dock Co. Ltd. Middlesbrough. Yard no. 1246.

Name Unchanged:
Scrapped in 1978.

First Diesel Electric trawler built for Hull fleet.

Diesel electric trawler.
2 oil 2DA each 7 cyl.
1886 brake horse power.
Driving 3 generators connected to electric motor 1500 shaft horse power.
Engines built by English Electric Co. Preston.

mt ST. DOMINIC H116

Gross tons: 829	Net Tons: 302
Length: 189'5"	Breadth: 34'5"

Owner:
Thomas Hamling & Co. Ltd. Hull.

Built:
1958 by Cook, Welton & Gemmell at Beverley. Yard no. 925.

Name Unchanged:
Scrapped in 1979.

Diesel electric trawler.
3 oil 4SA each 8 cyl.
220 brake horse power.
Driving 3 generators connected to 2 electric motors each 800 shaft horse power.
Engines built by Mirrlees, Bickerton & Day, Stockport.

mt PRINCE CHARLES H77

Gross tons: 691	Net Tons: 247
Length: 180'1"	Breadth: 32'9"

Owner:
St. Andrew's Steam Fishing Co. Ltd. Hull.

Built:
1958 by Cook, Welton & Gemmell at Beverley. Yard no. 929.

Name Unchanged:
Scrapped in 1978.

Motor trawler.
Oil 4SA.
1545 brake horse power.
Engine built by Werkspoor = C. D. Holmes, Hull.

Won Silver Cod Challenge Trophy 1960 with skipper B. Wharam.

mt STELLA LEONIS H322

Gross tons: 775	Net Tons: 267
Length: 189'7"	Breadth: 33'6"

Owners:
Charleson-Smith Trawlers Ltd. Hull (Ross Group).

Built:
1960 by Cook, Welton & Gemmell, at Beverley. Yard no. 944.

Renamed:
Ross Leonis 1965.
Scrapped in 1978.

Motor trawler.
Oil 4SA 6 cyl.
1800 brake horse power.
Engine built by Mirrlees, Bickerton & Day, Stockport.

Won Silver Cod Challenge Trophy 1963 and 1964 with skipper R. Waller.

mt ARCTIC CORSAIR H320

Gross tons: 776   Net tons: 256   Length 191'7"   Breadth: 33'11"

Owner: Boyd Line Ltd. Hull.

Built: 1960 by Cook, Welton & Gemmell at Beverley. Yard no. 959.

Sold in 1993 to Hull City Council for use as a museum ship.

Name Unchanged: Motor trawler.   1800 brake horse power.
                                       Oil 4SA 6 cyl.   Engine built by Mirrlees, Bickerton & Day, Stockport.

mt SOMERSET MAUGHAM H329

Gross tons: 789   Net Tons: 275

Length: 189'7"   Breadth: 33'11"

Owner:

Newington Steam Trawling Co. Ltd. Hull.

Built:

1961 by Cook, Welton & Gemmell at Beverley. Yard no. 965.

Name Unchanged:

Scrapped in 1978.

Motor trawler.

Oil 4SA 10 cyl.

2000 brake horse power.

Engine built by C. D. Holmes, Hull.

Won Silver Cod Challenge Trophy 1962, 1965, 1966 with skipper W. Brettell.

mt CAPE OTRANTO H227

Gross tons: 823   Net Tons: 237

Length: 193'8"   Breadth: 34'5"

Owners:

Hudson Brothers Trawlers (Ross Group).

Built:

1962 by Cook, Welton & Gemmell, at Beverley. Yard no. 972.

Renamed:

Ross Otranto 1965.

Scrapped in 1979.

Diesel electric trawler.

3 oil 4SA each 8 cyl.

2775 brake horse power.

Driving 3 generators connected to 2 electric motors each 850 shaft horse power.

Engines built by Mirrlees, Bickerton & Day, Stockport.

mt LORD NELSON H330

Gross tons: 1226   Net tons: 527   Length 221'7"   Breadth: 36'5"

Owner: West Dock Steam Fishing Co. Ltd. (Associated Fisheries).

Built: 1961 by Rickmers Werft, Bremerhaven. Yard no. 298. First stern trawler built for the Hull fleet.

Scrapped in 1981.   Motor stern trawler.   2000 brake horse power.

Oil 4SA 6 cyl.   Engine built by Mirrlees, Bickerton & Day, Stockport.

mt LORD JELLICOE H228

Gross tons: 596	Net Tons: 224
Length: 166′5″	Breadth: 30′5″

Owner:
Lord Line Ltd. Hull, (Associated Fisheries).

Built:
1962 by Cook, Welton & Gemmell at Beverley. Yard no. 979.

Renamed:
St. Louis 1982
Converted to an oil rig standby vessel in 1983. Still in service.

Motor trawler.
Oil 4SA 8 cyl.
1400 brake horse power.
Engines built by Mirrlees, Bickerton & Day, Stockport.

mt JUNELLA H347

Gross tons: 1435	Net Tons: 558
Length: 240′7″	Breadth: 38′7″

Owners:
J. Marr & Son Ltd. Hull.

Built:
1962 by Hall Russell & Co. Ltd. Aberdeen. Yard no. 900.

Renamed:
Bluefin 1973-1977 (South Africa)
Southern Ranger 1977 (Caymen Islands)
Now laid up in South Africa.

Diesel electric stern trawler.
3 oil 4SA each 8 cyl.
3237 brake horse power driving 3 generators connected to electric motor 2100 shaft horse power.
Engines built by English Electric Co. Newton le Willows.

mt CAPE KENNEDY H353

Gross tons: 1156   Net Tons: 531
Length: 226'6"   Breadth: 36'7"

Owner:
Hudson Brothers Trawlers Ltd. (Ross Group).

Built:
1965 by Cochrane & Sons Ltd. at Selby. Yard no. 1490.

Renamed:
Ross Kennedy 1966
Ross Intrepid 1966-1975
Malene Ostervold 1975 (Norway)
Converted to Seismographic survey ship in 1978.

Motor stern trawler.
Oil 4SA 9 cyl.
2150 brake horse power.
Engine built by Ruston & Hornsby, Lincoln.

mt LADY PARKES H397

Gross tons: 1746   Net Tons: 690
Length: 240'3"   Breadth: 41'1"

Owner:
Boston Deep Sea Fisheries Ltd. Hull.

Built:
1966 by Hall Russell & Co. Ltd. at Aberdeen. Yard no. 929.

Renamed:
Resolution 1977-1985 (French)
Odys-Echo 1985-1987
Odysse 1987
Converted to a geophysical-seismographic research vessel in 1977.

Motor stern trawler.
Oil 4SA 8 cyl.
2350 brake horse power.
Engines built by Mirrlees, National, Stockport.

mt CORIOLANUS H412

Gross tons: 1105	Net Tons: 360
Length: 223'9"	Breadth: 39'1"

Owner:
Hellyer Brothers Ltd. Hull.

Built:
1967 by Yarrow & Co. Ltd. Glasgow. Yard no. 2270.

Renamed:
Achaios 1980 (Greek)
Stratos S 1981 (Honduras)
Still in service as a trawler.

Motor stern trawler.
Oil 4SA 8 cyl.
2350 brake horse power.
Engine built by Mirrlees National, Stockport.

mt ARCTIC BUCCANEER H188

Gross tons: 1660	Net Tons: 793
Length: 280'6"	Breadth: 42'9"

Owners:
Boyd Line Ltd. Hull.

Built:
1973 by Stocznia Im Komuny Paraskiej at Gydnia. Yard no. B420-1.

Renamed:
Otago Buccaneer 1982 (New Zealand)
Ming Fu 1993 (China).
Still in service as a trawler. Largest class of trawler built for Hull owner.

Motor stern trawler.
Oil 4SA 8 cyl.
4000 brake horse power.
Engine built by Zgoda Sultzer Swietochlowiċe.

CHAPTER 4
POST WAR HULL TRAWLER LOSSES

Due to the hazardous nature of their work it was inevitable that trawler losses would occur. The Hull deepwater fishing fleet worked in some of the most hostile seas in the world, those of the North Atlantic and Arctic Oceans.

The main causes of the losses were:

Sailing in close proximity to land with visibility hampered by thick fog and blizzards or out at sea in storm force winds and freezing weather conditions.

Taking into account the size of the fleet and the number of days that trawlers spent away at sea the losses were relatively light. This bears testimony to the highly skilled seamanship of Hull trawler crews.

As well as the men lost with their ships hundreds of others were lost overboard or died from injury or illness. This chapter of the book is dedicated to their memory.

List of Post War Hull Trawler Losses

	Loch Hope	H220	1947		*Stella Rigel*	H170	1962
	St. Amandus	H247	1947	*	*Kingston Turquoise*	H50	1965
*	*Spaniard*	H366	1949		*St. Finbarr*	H308	1966
*	*St. Leander*	H19	1951	*	*St. Romanus*	H223	1968
	Norman	H289	1952	*	*Kingston Peridot*	H591	1968
	St. Ronan	H86	1952		*Ross Cleveland*	H61	1968
	Kingston Aquamarine	H520	1954	*	*James Barrie*	H15	1969
*	*Lorella*	H455	1955	*	*Caesar*	H226	1971
*	*Roderigo*	H135	1955	*	*St. Chad*	H20	1973
	Stella Orion	H379	1955		*Ian Fleming*	H396	1973
**	*Prince Charles*	H249	1955		*Gaul*	H243	1974
*	*St. Celestin*	H233	1956	**	*D. B. Finn*	H332	1975
	Staxton Wyke	H479	1959				
*	*St. Hubert*	H142	1960	*	*Photo*		
*	*Arctic Viking*	H452	1961	**	*Wreck salvaged and returned to Hull.*		

SPANIARD H366

Gross tons: 542   Net tons: 220
Length 167'1"   Breadth: 28'1"
Built: 1942 at Beverley as HMT *Dunkery* renamed *Spaniard* 1946.
Owned by: Hellyer Bros.
Wrecked 22.3.1949 off Sletnes Lighthouse, near Gamvik, Finnmark, North Norway. All the crew were saved.

ST. LEANDER H19

Gross tons: 658   Net Tons: 232
Length: 181'7"   Breadth: 30'8"
Built: 1949 at Beverley.
Owned by: Thomas Hamling & Co. Ltd.
Lost 9.1.1951 in the Humber. Whilst manoeuvring off St. Andrew's Dock the *St. Leander* collided with the Hull trawler *Davy* which was at anchor. She then drifted up to Barton Ness and was taken in tow, but she grounded at Hessle Flats. *St. Leander* was a new ship but unfortunately could not be salvaged and the wreck was blown up. All the crew were saved.

LORELLA H455

Gross tons: 559   Net Tons: 202
Length: 170'8"   Breadth: 30'8"
Built: 1947 at Beverley.
Owned by: J. Marr & Son Ltd.
See Loss details with *Roderigo*.

RODERIGO H135 (seen as built)

Gross tons: 810   Net Tons: 289
Length: 189'1"   Breadth: 32'2"
Built: 1950 at Beverley as *Princess Elizabeth*, renamed *Roderigo* 1951.
Owned by: Hellyer Bros.

Lost 26.1.1955 ninety miles north-east of the North Cape, Iceland. On 23.1.1955 *Roderigo* was steaming in company with *Lorella* because Lorella's radar had broken down. Most ships were sheltering at Riter Huk but *Lorella* and *Roderigo* moved out to assist the *Kingston Garnet* caught in the bad weather with a fouled propeller which her crew eventually managed to free (24.1.1955) and reach shelter. The *Lorella* and *Roderigo* were caught in severe gale force winds and freezing weather. Unable to turn for shelter the trawlers had to dodge into the wind, and after fighting severe weather for three days, they were overwhelmed by the build up of ice and capsized on 26.1.1955. Forty crewmen were lost.

ST. CELESTIN H233

Gross tons: 790   Net tons: 287
Length 188'5"   Breadth: 32'2"

Built: 1952 at Beverley.

Owned by: Thomas Hamling & Co. Ltd.

Lost 27.5.1956 after a collision with the Hull trawler *Arctic Viking* at Bear Island. Even though the sea was calm she sank within five minutes. All the crew were saved. The *Arctic Viking* was also lost in tragic circumstances in 1961.

ST. HUBERT H142

Gross tons: 568   Net Tons: 199
Length: 178'1"   Breadth: 28'7"

Built: 1950 at Kiel as *Ellerbek*, Renamed *St. Hubert* 1957.

Owned by: St. Andrew's Steam Fishing Co. Ltd.

Lost 29.8.1960 off Norway, when a five-foot cylinder which had been trawled up three days earlier and stowed to dump in deep water exploded; three of the crew were killed instantly and skipper Ness was fatally injured. The trawler, her foredeck wrecked and hatches blown out, had to run before a force eight gale, but after six hours she was abandoned and sank. The Hull trawler *Prince Charles* which had stood by her picked up the survivors.

ARCTIC VIKING H452

Gross tons: 533	Net Tons: 203
Length: 166'7"	Breadth: 27'6"

Built: 1937 at Selby as *Arctic Pioneer*, renamed *Arctic Viking* 1946.

Owned by: Boyd Line Ltd.

Lost 18.10.1961 sixteen miles off Flamborough Head. She capsized in a severe gale whilst homeward bound. Survivors were picked up by the Polish lugger *Derkacz*; five crewmen were lost.

KINGSTON TURQUOISE H50

Gross tons: 811	Net Tons: 288
Length: 189'4"	Breadth: 32'1"

Built: 1955 at Beverley.

Owned by: Kingston Steam Trawling Co. Ltd. (Hellyer Bros).

Wrecked 26.1.1965 on a sandbank about 14 miles NNW of Hoy Head, Orkney Islands. Although she managed to clear the sandbank the engine room crew found she was rapidly flooding and the crew abandoned ship, just before she sank; all this happened within a few minutes and one crewman was lost.

ST. ROMANUS H223

Gross tons: 599   Net Tons: 218
Length: 170'2"   Breadth: 29'2"
Built: 1950 at Beverley as *Van Dyck,* renamed *St. Romanus* 1964.
Owned by: Thomas Hamling & Co. Ltd.

Lost on or about 11.1.1968. Disappeared on passage to the Norwegian coast, during bad weather conditions. The mate of an Icelandic trawler reported he heard a May Day on 11.1.68 and later a raft and lifebuoy were found; 20 crewmen were lost.

KINGSTON PERIDOT H591

Gross tons: 658   Net Tons: 232
Length: 181'7"   Breadth: 30'8"
Built: 1948 at Beverley.
Owned by: Kingston Steam Trawling Co. Ltd. (Hellyer Bros).

Lost 26 or 27.1.1968. Capsized in bad weather conditions off Koposkar, North Iceland. She was heading home and had arranged on the 26th to rendezvous with *Kingston Sardius* on the Kiolsen Bank and she did not arrive; 20 crewmen were lost.

ROSS CLEVELAND H61

Gross tons: 659   Net Tons: 237
Length: 178'1"   Breadth: 30'1"

Built: 1949 at Aberdeen as *Cape Cleveland*, renamed *Ross Cleveland* 1965.

Owned by: Ross Group Ltd.

Lost 4.2.1968 whilst sheltering in Isafjordur in NW Iceland, three miles off Arnanes Light. Capsized and sank in exceptionally bad weather conditions; 18 crewmen were lost, only one man was saved.

CAESAR H226

Gross tons: 830   Net Tons: 317
Length: 189'5"   Breadth: 32'2"

Built: 1952 at Middlesbrough.

Owned by: Hellyer Brothers.

Wrecked 21.4.1971 at Arnanes at the entrance of Isafjord, whilst going into Isafjordur for repairs to the winch; all the crew were saved. She was refloated on 20.5.1971 but was badly damaged. Due to there being no shipbreakers in Iceland she was towed out to sea to be sunk 300 miles off Iceland; but she sank prematurely, 39 miles off the Icelandic coast on 1.6.1971.

JAMES BARRIE H15

| Gross tons: 666 | Net tons: 235 | Length 180'5" | Breadth: 30'4" |

Built: 1949 at Aberdeen as *Benella*, renamed *James Barrie* 1951.   **Owned by:** Newington Steam Trawling Co. Ltd.

Wrecked 27.3.1969 on Louther Skerry, Pentland Firth, whilst outward bound for Iceland. Her crew were rescued by Wick lifeboat. On 29th at high tide she slid free of the reef and was taken in tow by two lobster boats and pumps put on board were operated by Kirkwall lifeboat crew. But she sank 1½ miles off Hoxa Head just 10 miles from where it was hoped to beach her. All crew were saved.

mt ST. CHAD H20

Gross tons: 575	Net Tons: 210
Length: 165'3"	Breadth: 30'5"

Built: 1956 at Beverley.

Owned by: St. Andrew's Steam Fishing Co. Ltd.

Wrecked 30.3.1973 at Ritur Huk at the entrance of Isafjord in a blizzard and severe gales, whilst shelting with a large fleet of British trawlers. Her crew were rescued by the support ship *Othello*. All the crew were saved.

mt D B FINN H332

Gross tons: 701	Net Tons: 236
Length: 188'0"	Breadth: 32'7"

Built: 1961 at Goole.

Owned by: Boston Deep Sea Fisheries Ltd.

Grounded 21.3.1975 near Cape Hjorleif-shofdi on Iceland's south coast, during hurricane force gales. All 21 crewmen were rescued. The *D B Finn* was refloated and returned to Hull. But it was decided she was too costly to repair and so on 10.6.1975 she sailed for Blyth where she was scrapped.

LOSSES: WITHOUT PHOTOGRAPHS

LOCH HOPE H220

| Gross tons: 274 | Net tons: 109 |
| Length: 133'5" | Breadth: 22'7" |

Built: 1915 at Beverley as *Princess Marie José*.
Owned by: Loch Fishing Co. Ltd.
Renamed:
Feughside 1939-1946
Loch Hope 1946
Lost 11.6.1947 off East Iceland when a mine which had caught in the nets exploded, causing serious damage to the ship which sank. Eight crewmen were injured and one killed.

ST. AMANDUS H247

| Gross tons: 443 | Net tons: 164 |
| Length: 162'1" | Breadth: 26'7" |

Built: 1934 at Middlesbrough as *Loch Melfort*.
Owned by: Thomas Hamling & Co. Ltd.
Renamed:
St. Amandus 1946
Lost Wrecked 24.12.1947 at Skrova in Vesfjord near the Lofoten Islands, Norway, during gales. All crew were saved.

NORMAN H289

| Gross tons: 629 | Net tons: 242 |
| Length: 178'5" | Breadth: 29'2" |

Built: 1943 at Beverley HMT *Bombardier*.
Owned by: Hellyer Brothers Ltd.
Renamed:
Norman 1946
Wrecked 4.10.1952 on Skerries East of Cape Farewell, South Greenland, in thick fog. As the ship listed the crew tried to swim ashore. Twenty men were lost, only one man saved (by coincidence his name happened to be Norman).

ST. RONAN H86

| Gross tons: 568 | Net tons: 206 |
| Length: 170'2" | Breadth: 29'2" |

Built: 1948 at Beverley as *Princess Elizabeth*.
Owned by: Thomas Hamling Co. Ltd.
Renamed:
St. Ronan 1949
Wrecked 12.10.1952 at St. John's Point, Caithness, Scotland, whilst outward bound for Greenland. All the crew were saved.

KINGSTON AQUAMARINE H520

| Gross tons: 613 | Net tons: 232 |
| Length: 180'1" | Breadth: 30'2" |

Built: 1948 at Aberdeen as *St. Mark*.
Owned by: Kingston Steam Trawling Co. Ltd.
Renamed:
Kingston Aquamarine in 1952
Wrecked 11.1.1954 on rock on the West Side of Senja Island, north of the Lofoten Islands, Norway. All the crew were saved.

STELLA ORION H379

| Gross tons: 575 | Net tons: 228 |
| Length: 178'1" | Breadth: 30'0" |

Built: 1943 at Beverley as HMT *Lancer*.
Owned by: Charleson-Smith Trawlers Ltd.
Renamed:
Stella Orion 1946
Wrecked 7.11.1955 at Vestfjorden, North Norway, whilst homeward bound from the Barents Sea. All the crew were saved.

PRINCE CHARLES H249

| Gross tons: 514 | Net tons: 184 |
| Length: 161'1" | Breadth: 29'1" |

Built: 1953 at Selby.
Owned by: St. Andrew's Steam Fishing Co. Ltd.
Wrecked 23.12.1955. Ran aground on the Island of Socroeya 60 miles west of Hammerfest, during a snowstorm. The survivors were rescued from the shore, by the Norwegian ship *Ingoey* after two hours. Nine crewmen and one Norwegian pilot were lost. The wreck was salvaged and was towed back to Hull, where she arrived on 3.10.1956. She was repaired and became *Loch Melfort*. To Fleetwood 1965 and scrapped 1976.

STAXTON WYKE H479

| Gross tons: 472 | Net tons: 177 |
| Length: 177'0" | Breadth: 27'2" |

Built: 1937 at Beverley as *Lady Hogarth*.
Owned by: West Dock Steam Fishing Co. Ltd.
Renamed:
Kingston Emerald 1946
Staxton Wyke 1951
Lost 23.8.1959, nine miles east of Hornsea. Whilst homeward bound from Iceland steaming in thick fog she was in collision with 11,000 ton Newcastle ore-carrier *Dalhanna*. Almost cut in two she sank in under two minutes. Five crewmen were lost.

STELLA RIGEL H170

| Gross tons: 568 | Net tons: 266 |
| Length: 170'0" | Breadth: 29'2" |

Built: 1949 at Beverley as *Princes Philip*.

Owned by: Charleson-Smith Trawlers Ltd.

Renamed:
Hargood (Grimsby) 1955-1958
Stella Rigel 1958

Wrecked 21.12.1962. Ran aground near Toravaac lighthouse off the north sea of Norway whilst outward bound. Crew took to life rafts and were picked up by Norwegian fishing vessel *Siv*. All the crew were saved.

mt ST. FINBARR H308

| Gross tons: 1139 | Net tons: 505 |
| Length: 210'6" | Breadth: 36'4" |

Built: 1964 at Port Glasgow.

Owned by: Thomas Hamling & Co. Ltd.

On 25 December 1966 a fire broke out in the accommodation area. This rapidly spread to the bridge and skipper Sawyers gave orders to prepare to abandon ship. The thirteen survivors were rescued by the Hull trawler *Orsino* which took the striken *St. Finbarr* in tow. She sank on 27 December 1966, twelve crew were lost.

mt IAN FLEMING H396

| Gross tons: 598 | Net tons: 204 |
| Length: 176'6" | Breadth: 32'7" |

Built: 1958 at Beverley as *Fylkir* (Icelandic).

Owned by: Newlington Steam Trawling Co. Ltd.

Renamed:
Ian Fleming 1966

Wrecked 30.3.1973 off Havoysund 20 miles south-west of the North Cape whilst outward bound for the northerly grounds off Norway. She finally sank on 5 January 1974; 17 crewmen were saved, but three were lost.

mt GAUL H243

| Gross tons: 1106 | Net tons: 411 |
| Length: 216'9" | Breadth: 40'2" |

Built: 1972 at Lowestoft as *Ranger Castor*.

Owned by: British United Trawlers Ltd.

Renamed:
Gaul 1973

Lost 8 February 1974. The *Gaul* went missing on 8 February 1974 whilst dodging in severe weather off the North Cape of Norway. It is thought that she capsized due to a build up of water on her factory deck or by being overwhelmed by freak waves. 36 crewmen were lost.

CHAPTER 5
TRAWLERS IN TROUBLE

Shortly after leaving St. Andrew's Dock outward bound for the fishing grounds on 14 February 1953, the trawler *Loch Torridon* H165 was involved in a collision with the m.v. *Emerald*. The *Loch Torridon* sustained considerable damage on her port side, being holed from the deck to below the water line. Whereupon her skipper E. March beached the stricken trawler between Victoria Dock and the Alexandra Dock Pier. By doing so he saved the trawler from foundering in deep water.

Two local tugs *Tollman* and *Boatman* went to her aid and a third tug *Pinky* arrived to assist in salvage operations.

The salvage of the trawler proved to be difficult. The workmen from St. Andrew's Engineering company were hampered by the sharp port list and 250 tons of coal had to be moved before repairs to the gash could start from the inside. Also they could only work at low tide because at high tide most of the ship was under water.

The *Loch Torridon* was successfully refloated on 20 March 1953 and after a refit was returned to sea.

Built in 1934 as the *Brimness* and renamed *Loch Torridon* in 1946 the trawler was scrapped in 1959.

The m.v. *Emerald* a 1382 gross ton 230ft long motor vessel, owned by W. Robertson of Glasgow, was only slightly damaged and was able to proceed up river.

Whilst outward bound for the Norwegian fishing grounds on 11 March 1959, the *Stella Carina* H573 was in collision with the collier *Mendip* in the River Humber off Victoria Dock.

The *Stella Carina* sustained a gash 22ft deep and 3ft wide in her port side and she began to sink by the stern. The quick thinking of skipper Fred Sullivan averted a tragedy. With chief engineer George Roberts working up to his waist in water in the engine room, the skipper turned the stricken trawler towards the shore and beached her near to Victoria Dock.

With the trawler sinking deeper in the water the 20 crew used inflatable life-rafts to get clear of the ship and they were picked up by a pilot cutter, which had witnessed the accident.

The *Mendip* a 1362 gross ton 235ft collier owned by Wm. Cory & Son of London was slightly damaged by the collision but was able to proceed to Goole.

It took over two months to salvage the trawler but on 27 May 1959 the *Stella Carina* was towed back to St. Andrew's Dock. After a lengthy stay in dock for major repairs the trawler returned to sea in September 1959.

Built in 1948 at Selby as the *St. Christopher* H573 became *Tesla* in 1949 and *Stella Carina* in 1955. The trawler was scrapped in 1967.

The *Stella Canopus* H244 had been on the slip for a survey and was refloated on Saturday afternoon, 22 January 1949. Broady's had taken away the main discharge valve for refurbishing and were due to refit it on the Sunday morning. Although this left a hole in the trawler's side a foot above the waterline this in normal circumstances represented no danger to the trawler.

The *Stella Canopus* was moored on dryside in the extension dock near to the 'mechanic' coal crane. During the course of time as trawlers were loaded with coal some of it dropped into the dock and a sill had formed beneath where the trawler was placed.

On Sunday morning a large number of trawlers entered the dock for the Monday morning market. This meant keeping the lockgates open for quite some time and the water level in the dock fell to a low level.

This caused the *Stella Canopus* to come down on to the sill and list over; water then entered the trawler, causing her to capsize.

Two crews of the fish dock tugs *Bernie* and *Kiero* witnessed what was happening and came alongside the stricken trawler to prevent her falling completely over. In addition, the fish dock water boat came alongside to prop up the trawler.

Meanwhile repair workers from Humber St. Andrews Engineering Company who were working on another vessel went on board the *Stella Canopus* to help fix wires ashore to hold the trawler up.

Gradually with the aid of pumps from the tug and the lines ashore the trawler was brought back upright.

By this time workers from Broady's had come down the dock with the missing valve and as the water level in the engine room was reduced it was possible to refit the valve.

The trawler was then floated clear of the sill and returned to the slip where she was inspected for damage, and repaired. After the repairs were completed the trawler returned to sea.

Built in 1946 as the *Northella* and renamed *Stella Canopus* in 1948 the trawler was scrapped in 1967.

On 13 November 1966 the trawler *St. Amant* H42 capsized on top of an oil barge in St. Andrew's Dock.

The accident happened as the trawler was being prepared for dry dock. On the previous Wednesday the *St. Amant* had returned to the dock after being damaged in a collision with the dredger *Skitterness* in the River Humber whilst outward bound for the fishing grounds in foggy weather. A hole was ripped in the trawler's starboard fuel tank and about 50 tons of fuel oil was lost. Some damage was also done to the bridge but no-one was injured.

The capsize occurred as oil was being pumped out of the port tank and the trawler lost stability when a mooring rope snapped.

On board the trawler were:- the night watchman, a steam raiser and three oilmen, and there were two crewmen on the barge. Fortunately no-one was hurt in the accident.

The three fish dock tugs: *Aurora, Tryton* and *Zephyr* were called to pull on the trawler with tackle and to pump water into the port tank.

For nearly 3 hours the *St. Amant* lay on her side at an angle of 45 degrees, until firemen manning pumps, the tugs and winchmen slowly righted her. After repairs she entered dry dock and eventually returned to sea.

Built in 1949 as the *Swanella* H42, and renamed *St. Amant* in 1952 the trawler was scrapped in 1973.

CHAPTER 6
TRAWLERMEN AT WORK

A trawlerman joins his ship about an hour prior to the vessel sailing. The kit bag slung over his shoulder will contain his working clothes and another bag a few luxuries from home or the ship's stores: books, sweets and fruit.

It is difficult to explain to "shoreside" people the mixed emotions a seaman feels when rejoining a ship, but going back to work after a really good holiday must come close.

This unusual low level photograph taken from a boat moored to the landing stage, shows the *St. Loman* H156 heading out of the lockpit of St. Andrew's Dock at the beginning of her trip.

In the early morning gloom only a few friends of the crew and the ship's husband and runner are on the dockside to shout farewells.

The *St. Loman* at 895 gross tons was the biggest side-fishing trawler built for British owners.

In the days before domestic fridges were installed on trawlers, the crew's meat rations were stored on the top of the ice in the fish room. In some trawlers it was the custom to "salt" a few beef and pork joints in brine casks which were situated on the boat deck.

In this photograph the crew are checking the quality of the meat the ship's chandler has provided and one of the better joints has been selected for dinner.

The skipper uses a sextant to check the trawler's position with the midday sun. Modern navigational aids have all but made this instrument a museum piece.

This is the radio room with the wireless operator tapping a message on the morse key.
The wireless operator provided the crew with the vital link to the outside world, transmitting and receiving information
between the owner's office, other trawlers in the fleet and the all important telegrams
between crews and their families at home.

One of the most important members of a ship's crew was the cook. His ability could make or break a ship. Once a trawler started fishing, good wholesome food and a half-hour break in the warmth of the messroom was all the deck crew had to look forward to, to break up the 18 hour working day.

The cook was relied upon to turn out hot food even when the trawler was moving wildly about in stormy weather. Hanging onto your seat at the table and eating it was another matter.

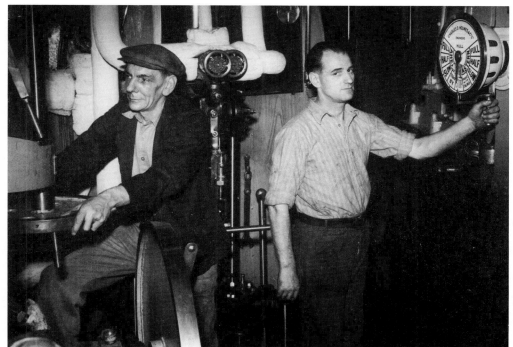

The Chief Engineer and his fireman at the controls of an oil-fired steam trawler in the 1950's. Working in tandem with the 2nd Engineer and his fireman, the engine-room crew needed great skill and expertise to keep the trawler engines working non-stop for up to 21 days, the normal length of a trip for a deep water side-fishing trawler.

A deckhand at work with needle and twine preparing the trawl net, whilst the trawler is outward bound to the fishing grounds.

Teamwork is the name of the game as the deckies wait for the ship to roll back to starboard (right) to clear the heavy bobbins over the side prior to shooting the trawl.

Deckies inspect the wings of the trawl as it is brought inboard to check for holes or damage through which the fish will escape.

The fish caught in the trawl are pushed down into the cod-end which is then emptied into the pounds. On this occasion there is not much to show for a 4 hour tow.

This shot shows a much better haul of codling, ling and catfish. The main task of the deckies is to clear this lot before the next haul. The fact that they are wearing caps instead of sou-westers is an indication that there is a spell of good weather. The basket is for the cod livers which will be taken to the liver house to be boiled to extract the cod liver oil.

This view of the foredeck taken from the bridge shows how exposed the crew of a sidewinder were to the wind and sea. After being gutted the fish are thrown into the washer which is situated in the centre of the hatches.

Another important member of the crew is the fishroom man. His expertise in storing the fish is crucial to the success of the trip. The fish is laid on top of a layer of ice and then shelf-boards are placed over them to prevent the fish from being crushed. This process known as shelving is reserved for the best fish like cod or haddock. Less valuable species were stored in bulk pounds.

The liver house was situated in the stern of the ship. It was here that the livers were brought to be "boiled" in the large vats to extract the cod-liver oil. Once cooked the oil was sieved and it passed into a storage tank from which it was pumped into a tanker barge back at Hull and taken to the local refinery.

The job of boiling the livers was traditionally that of the radio operator. The money raised from the sale of the oil was paid out amongst the crew.

The trawler *Macbeth* H113 arrives safely back at St. Andrew's Dock. After passing through the lockpits the trawler will be berthed on the fish quay where her catch will be auctioned at the early morning market. As the crew head home they will be gripped with the excitement of the prospect of 2 days at home and hopefully a good cash settlement.

Once a trawler arrived back in Hull, everyone was in a hurry to get home.

In this 1950's photograph a Customs officer is coming down the ladder from the bridge to tell the skipper that he has checked the manifest and sealed the bond locker, and so the ship is cleared.

The man coming up the ladder will be eagerly waiting to be told that the crew can get off home.

The skipper's wife who has come down to the dock to meet him will be updating him on family matters and enquiring if he has had a good trip. A frequent story in the popular press of those days was a feature on "super-tax skippers" who were among the country's top earners.

CHAPTER 7

PHOTOGRAPHIC SURVEY OF ST. ANDREW'S DOCK

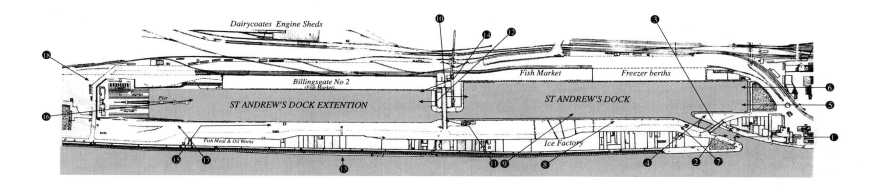

PLAN OF ST ANDREW'S DOCK
(1897-1975)

This elevated view of the entrance to St. Andrew's Dock, dates back to 1955. On the peak of high water the two lock gates were opened to allow vessels to sail straight out of — or into the dock.

The lock was 250' long, 50' wide and the depth at high water on ordinary spring tides was 29'10".

Leading the ships through the locks out into the River Humber is Hellyer Brothers' trawler *Man-O-War* H181. Judging by the immaculate condition of her paint-work the trawler has just undergone a survey.

Map ref. 1.

A large crowd gathers on the dockside to welcome home the crew of the *Lord Nelson* H330, when the trawler arrived home from her maiden voyage in August 1961.

Commanded by skipper Walter Lewis with a crew of 24, the *Lord Nelson* was Hull's first stern-fishing trawler.

Built for Associated Fisheries by Rickmers Werft, Bremerhaven, as an experimental stern trawler. The *Lord Nelson* had two fish rooms, the idea being to fill the frozen fish room first, then store the normal fresh fish catch in the second fish room.

The *Lord Nelson* proved to be a success and soon other trawler owners placed orders for stern trawlers. Only a few more traditional side-fishing trawlers were built for the Hull fleet, the last of these completed in 1963.

Map ref. 3.

Trawlers usually entered St. Andrew's Dock stern first, to avoid having to be turned in the confined space of the dock.
But late arrivals which would have to "pen" into the dock using the locks due to the low level of water
were allowed to come in bow first. This was to save valuable time manoeuvering off the dock.
In this 1959 photograph, members of the crew of the *Loch Moidart* chat to shore workers alongside the Dock Master's office
whilst they wait for the lock gates to close behind them.
Map ref. 2.

Once trawlers had been prepared for sea they were placed near to the lock entrance ready to sail on the next tide.
At the east end of the dock on 26 March 1959 are left to right:
Stella Sirius H165, *Cape Spartel* H79, *Olvina* H139 and *Stella Antares* H123.
The inner trawler *Lord Tedder* H154 is undergoing a survey.
Two of the fish dock tugs are on standby ready to tow the outward-bound trawlers into the locks.
Map ref. 4.

This view looking down the length of St. Andrew's Dock facing west was taken from the Lord Line building in 1953.

It shows the outline of the original dock which opened in 1883. The water area was 1,901 feet long and 250 feet wide.

The buildings to the left consist of trawler owners' offices, ship repair shops, Stanton's Café, and the Ice Factory. To the right is the North Sea fish market.

In 1953 there were 161 trawlers in the Hull deep water fleet, 60 were coal-burners, 96 oil-fired and 5 motor trawlers. Map ref. 5.

By the time this picture was taken on 26 February 1968, 17 freezer stern trawlers were operating out of Hull. The three freezers on the right are berthed at the new No. 1 quay where the catches of frozen fish were unloaded into lorries for transportation to the local cold stores.

The *St. Jason* H436 had just completed her maiden voyage. Also to be seen are two of the "water tractors" which replaced the old steam tugs.

The North Sea "seiner" moving down the dock is *Nordborg* H35, one of a number of such vessels which were based in Hull over the years. Locally known as "snibbies". Map ref. 6.

This view was taken from the roof of the St. Andrew's Steam Fishing Company building on 28 March 1956.
To the left are a large number of taxis and cars, which will have brought trawler crews down to the dock to collect their settling money.
In this area were situated the offices of several trawler owners. These were:-
Loch Fishing Co. Ltd., Henriksen & Co. Ltd., Hudson Brothers Trawlers Ltd., Thomas Hamling & Co. Ltd., Hellyer Brothers Ltd., and Charleson-Smith Trawlers Ltd.
Trawlers berthed on the dryside include:- *St. Britwin* H124, and *Lorenzo* H230. On the North Sea market are:-
Cape Campbell H383, *Brucella* H291 and *St. Amant* H42.
The gap in the market behind the *St. Amant* is where the dockside collapsed on 4 April 1956.
Map ref. 7.

This view facing east towards the dock entrance was taken in 1953.

The three trawlers in the centre of the picture are being prepared for sea. Having taken on a fresh supply of crushed ice the trawlers are taking on stores, undergoing last minute repairs and also receiving a coat of paint.

On the day before the trawler sailed the ship's chandler would deliver the provisions the cook had ordered.

The crane was used to lift heavy items of gear either onto or off the trawlers. The odd-looking craft coming along the dock behind the trawler's mast is one of the "Seven Seas" cod liver oil barges which pumped the oil out of the trawler's storage tanks prior to it being taken by road tanker to the Marfleet refinery.
Map ref. 8.

This view facing north east was taken from the roof of the ice factory on a Saturday morning in 1962.

The picture features the overhead conveyors which carried the crushed ice direct from the factory straight into the trawler's fishroom ice pounds.

Apart from a few workers carrying out essential duties, the majority of the fish dock work force would be at home spending the weekend relaxing.

On the skyline are the chimneys of some of the local fish curing premises. With around 50 smoke houses, Hull was the biggest fish curing port in Britain.

The six trawlers ready for sea on dryside are:- *Lord Alexander* H12, *Arctic Vandal* H344, *Benvolio* H22, *Falstaff* H107, *Cape Otranto* H227 and *Stella Procyon* H184. On the market are:- *Arctic Cavalier* H204, *St. Keverne* H158 and *Northella* H98.
Map ref. 9.

This tranquil scene at St. Andrew's Dock facing east towards the dock entrance and Lord Line building was taken on a Sunday in 1966.

By tradition British fishing boats returned to harbour on Sunday, this being the day of worship and rest.

At Hull this tradition was partly upheld in that trawlers rarely sailed after noon on Saturday and never on Sunday. The dock was of course named after the patron saint of fishermen.

This led to quite a build up of trawlers waiting to sail on the Monday morning tide. In this view 21 trawlers are berthed in the dock, 14 of which are ready for sea, so the Dock Master and his staff will have a busy time ahead of them.

In the early hours of Monday morning the tranquillity would be broken as the bobbers began work unloading the trawlers' catches onto the fish market.
Map ref. 10.

After unloading their catch on the Iceland market which was in the St. Andrew's Dock extension, trawlers had to be towed through to the servicing area alongside the ice factory.

Coming through the gap between the two sections of the dock is *Lord Fraser* H48. A swing bridge linked the two sides of the dock at this point.

The buildings to the right (northside) are the St. Andrew's Dock Chambers which housed the railway offices, Hull Fish Merchants' Club, the Post Office, Banks, fish merchants' offices and Cullen's refreshment rooms.
Map ref. 11.

This view of the St. Andrew's Dock extension facing west dates from 1956.

Built for the North Eastern Railway Company and opened in 1897, the extension doubled the water area of the fish dock to over 19 acres.

The length of dockside to the left was used for berthing trawlers which were in port for major repairs and surveys and therefore they were kept away from the dock's main activities. Trawlers which were laid up or waiting to be scrapped were moored near to the fish meal factory which was situated at the south-west corner of the dock.

To the right the fish dock tug *Bernie* is towing the unloaded trawler *Cape Portland* H357 through to St. Andrew's Dock dryside for taking on stores for the return to sea. The slipway was located at the far (west) end of the extension dock.   Map ref. 12.

This photograph of the St. Andrew's Dock extension was part of an aerial survey of the Hull docks which was carried out in 1954.
The view shows how well the land area of the dock estate was utilised.
On the southside the backs of the buildings came right up to the bank of the River Humber, also there are no gaps between them.
At the top of the picture are the Dairycoates engine sheds, which were the biggest in the north of England.
Express freight locomotives from the sheds were often rostered to haul the local fish trains.
Map ref. 13.

This view of the extension facing east towards the fish meal factory was taken from the roof of the St. Andrew's Dock Chambers in the summer of 1966.

During summer months the demand for fish declined, borne out by the fact that whilst a large number of trawlers are laid up for repair, only the *Starella* H219 is landing her catch on the market.

In 1966 the Associated Group decided to re-register its Hull fleet under the name of Hellyer Brothers and repaint them in that company's livery.

Already shorn of its Kingston Steam Trawling Company colours is the *Kingston Peridot* H591 (left). Waiting their turn are *Kingston Sapphire* H95, *Newby Wyke* H111, *Kingston Beryl* H128 and *Kingston Pearl* H127.

On the dockside three former "Capes" are receiving Ross Group colours, and astern are two of Thomas Hamling's ex-Belgian trawlers, four of which were acquired in 1964.
Map ref. 14.

This view of the dockside facing east was taken from alongside the fish meal factory on 1 June 1965.

Alongside the trawler undergoing survey are four welding plants belonging to Humber St. Andrew's Engineering Company, who were the main repair company based at St. Andrew's Dock.

Under United Kingdom regulations all vessels have to be maintained to the highest standards and are required to complete regular surveys.

This work involved some unpleasant jobs for the ship repair workforce. Welders had to enter cramped vile smelling waste tanks to repair cracks and leaks, also boiler scalers had to crawl into the boilers to clean them out.

Once all the jobs had been carried out to the satisfaction of all concerned, the trawler was repainted and returned to sea in pristine condition.
Map ref. 15.

This view of the extension dock fish market was taken from the end of the slipway pier in 1950.

Although the docks were nationalised on 1 January 1948 the new owners, the British Transport Docks Board, were in no hurry to obliterate the name of the docks' previous owner. As is the case of the L.N.E.R. No. 2 Fish Quay.

This building dates back to the early 1930's when the London & North Eastern Railway Company had to reconstruct the Hull fish market following a disastrous fire which destroyed the previous No. 2 market on the evening of Sunday 25 August 1929.

The last trawler in the line is the ill-fated *St. Ronan* H86, which was wrecked at St. John's Point, Caithness, Scotland on 12 October 1952. Map ref. 16.

The St. Andrew's Dock slipway was located at the western end of the extension dock. An essential part of the dock's operation, the slipway could accommodate up to four vessels at a time.

As well as trawlers, tugs, coasters and pilot cutters all used the slipway's facilities.

Vessels were lifted from the water by the use of cradles which were mounted on tracks. To lift a vessel the cradle was lowered into the dock, then tugs manoeuvred the ship into position onto the cradle which was then hauled out of the dock by heavy winches.

Seen on the slip in November 1952 are (left) the *Todak*, a 299 gross ton — 129' long coastal tanker built by Henry Scarr at Hessle for the Shell Oil Company of Singapore. To the right are the trawlers *Lord Montgomery* H401 and the *Conan Doyle* H251.
Map ref. 17.

This view shows the slipway from the opposite direction to the previous photograph and dates from the early 1950's.

In the foreground are the rails on which the cradles ran and the heavy wire ropes which were used to haul them up the slipway.

When a ship was secured in position a large gangway was placed alongside and staging was placed on the hull for the repair workers to start their work.

Repairs carried out on the slipway were:- the propeller, rudder and bottom plates; also the lower part of the ship could be painted.

The *Langland Bay* SA72 was formerly the Hull trawler *Kingston Olivine*, which was built in 1930. The *Langland Bay* was owned by Swansea Trawlers Ltd., and while she was sailing out of Hull the trawler was managed by the Eton Steam Fishing Company.
Map ref. 18.

The larger, modern trawlers were sent to one of the local dry docks for major repairs and surveys.

The handiest of these dry docks was in William Wright Dock as this was located close to St. Andrew's Dock. If space was not available in this dock, trawlers were sent either to King George Dock or Alexandra Dock.

Undergoing survey in one of the Alexandra Dock drydocks is the *Lord Beatty* H112. Built in Germany in 1956 the *Lord Beatty* won the Silver Cod Challenge Trophy in 1957-1958 with skipper Walter Lewis. Considered one of the best trawlers built for the Hull fleet the *Lord Beatty* was one of ten Lord Line trawlers transferred to Grimsby in 1963.

This photograph along with the previous one highlights the graceful lines of the deep-water fishing trawler. Although considered by some to be just a work-horse of the seas, to the crews who sailed on them and many shipping enthusiasts the trawler is one of the finest looking vessels to grace the sea.

CHAPTER 8: FISH MARKET : WET SIDE

This elevated view of the fish market with the trawler *Stella Rigel* H170 landing her catch was taken on the afternoon of Wednesday 25 March 1959, which was the Holy Week "Showday".

Holy Week was the time of the year when fish landings attained their highest proportions. The Wednesday "Showday" was the day when the demand for fish for Good Friday reached its peak.

For "Showday" 1959, 15 trawlers and 3 seiners landed 26,500 10-stone kits of fish. All available space along the three-quarters of a mile length of the fish market was used to capacity, with 11 trawlers and the 3 seiners landing in the morning and the other 4 trawlers landing in the afternoon.

The bobbers started unloading at 2 a.m. and worked till late afternoon. Fish filleters worked from early morning till late evening.

Between 11 a.m. and 10.35 p.m. 11 fish trains left the Hull Fish Dock sidings for destinations throughout the country.

Landings for Holy Week 1959 were Monday 20,690 kits, Tuesday 23,000 kits, Wednesday 26,500 kits and Thursday 11,600 kits. The market was closed for the Easter Holidays.

The job of unloading the trawler's catch began at 2 a.m. and usually the work would be finished by 7 a.m. For every 300 kits of fish in the trawler's fish room, one gang of ten men was allocated. Normally 6-10 gangs would work each trawler.

From each gang, four "below men" worked down in the trawler's fish room. They took the fish and ice out of the storage pounds and sorted the different species into baskets. Once a basket was full it was winched out of the hold onto the dockside.

This photograph taken in 1951, shows the "below men" at work in the fish room and judging by the amount of clear space they have uncovered the job of unloading is almost finished.

The bobbers who worked on the trawler's deck next to the hatches were known as "swingers".
They worked in rhythm with a winchman ashore (he is the centre figure of the three men working near the upturned fish kits.)
Once the swinger had guided a basket of fish up out of the hatch, he swung the basket ashore to the "weigher off" (he is standing to the right).
As the basket was swung ashore the swinger would shout out what the contents of basket were i.e:- cod, haddock, colley, plaice etc.
This photograph of bobbers at work unloading a trawler was taken in 1965.

As the basket of fish was swung ashore the "weigher off" tipped the contents into a 10-stone fish kit,
which was placed on scales to check its weight. Then one of the "barrowmen" who can be seen waiting in the background
would take the kit to its place on the market, ready for the fish auction.
This photograph dates from 1965.

Another group of men who were employed in the unloading of the catch were the "board scrubbers". These men began work one hour after the bobbers.

As the trawler's fish pounds were emptied the pound boards were brought up on deck, where they were scrubbed clean of ice and fish residue. As the boards were cleaned they were neatly stacked out of the way until the unloading had been completed. The boards were then placed back in the fish room ready for the next supply of crushed ice.

This photograph of board scrubbers at work on the *Lord Howe* H19 was taken in 1957.

When it was unloaded the trawler's catch would be laid alongside the vessel in blocks of 40 kits, arranged in a set pattern according to type and size of fish. Cod was placed facing west towards the Iceland end of the market and haddock was placed facing east towards the North Sea market.

Plaice, coley, catfish, berguilts (reds) and others were placed on the foreshore.

This picture of a fish landing dates from March 1950.

The wooden fish kits were made by the coopers, Sutherland Tate, whose factory was in Hawthorn Avenue. In 1950 new aluminium kits were introduced and this led to the famous old firm of coopers closing down.

The kits are stamped with the initials of the Hull Trawler Supply Company who loaned them out.

This photograph of the trawler *Peter Cheyney* H195 and its catch laid out for the sale at the west end of the Iceland market, was taken on 25 March 1964.

The fish merchants and fish buyers normally arrived on the market at 6 a.m. to pick out the best fish which they would hope to buy. The buyers would check the quality of fish by smell, look and touch. The guidelines to buying fish were:-

Fresh fish has very little odour, the smell developing as the quality of the fish deteriorates. Newly caught fish is bright in colour with red gills; as time passes colour fades. Fresh fish is firm to touch; as it ages the texture becomes softer.

For the fish sale which began at 8 a.m. trawler owners had their own fish salesmen. One would sell cod, one would sell haddock, another would sell the oddments. The cod sale started at the west end of the Iceland market at Stand 204 and the haddock sale started at the opposite end of the North Sea market at Stand 1. The oddments were sold along with the cod. The salesmen and buyers moved along the market at quite a fast pace and as the kits of fish were sold the buyers tally label was placed on top to indicate ownership.

This view of the fish sale looking down from the gantry was taken in 1951.

Each merchant and his buyers would attend the different sales. The fish was sold by Dutch auction in blocks of 40 kits, beginning at say 100/- a kit. The price dropped until a buyer shouted "at". He then stated how many kits he wanted and then the salesman returned to the starting price until all the fish was sold.

In this photograph George Haikes, a fish salesman for Kingston Steam Trawling Company, is conducting a sale accompanied by his two booking-clerks.

Other people present are: Ken Kapron, Stan Branski, Bill Cox, Fred Sallonbank and Alf. Mason.

Once the fish was sold it had to be taken to the fish merchants' premises as quickly as possible so that the filleters could start work.

Fish dock transport played a vital role in the movement of the kits of fish around the market and also to the fish houses which were situated off the dock.

In this 1952 view of the landing stage on the north side of the market, most of the available parking space is taken up by carting agents' and fish merchants' lorries which are being loaded with fish.

The three cars to the right of the line of vehicles, are taxis waiting to collect crewmen from a docking trawler.

As the kits of fish were taken away to the buyers,
a space was cleared and the filleters' trays were brought out onto the market.
The men working on the dock edge had the worst position. On a sunny day it wasn't a bad job, but when it rained they got soaking wet.
For all the filleters working on the exposed fish market in winter, life was harsh. The water in the tray was freezing cold and the filleters' hands
became numb with cold. Plenty of hot drinks and snacks were needed to keep the job going.

Despite the primitive working conditions on the fish dock, the lads could always find something funny to have a laugh at.
Working as a team and discussing local topics helped the time pass more amiably.
Due to water and pieces of fish making the market surface very slippery,
the traditional wooden clogs were worn by everyone who worked on the fish market.
The main form of transport for the fish dock workers was the "push bike"! These were hung up out of the way until they were needed.
This view dates from 1951.

The finished product!! Boxes of top quality fish fillets are stacked ready for dispatching alongside the stand of Joe Robinson & Son on the Iceland market in 1961.

Many fishmongers and fish and chip shops ordered their fish direct from the merchants at Hull. The size of these orders varied from 40 boxes for a large concern at London's Billingsgate fish market to a single box of fillets for a shop at Middleton-on-the-Wolds.

Records show that even small orders for 2 boxes were delivered as far afield as:- Bournemouth, Chichester, Bexley Heath, Ebbw Vale, Abertillery, Gloucester, Colchester and Barnard Castle. So it would seem that no order was too small, or the distance involved too much trouble.

This is a view of the fish merchants' new offices on the North Sea market, which came into use in 1960. A 300 yard stretch of the market had to be rebuilt after it collapsed on 4 April 1956. The subsidence was the result of damage caused by a landmine during the 1939-45 War.

The fish boxes stored to the left are empty herring boxes from Bergen in Norway. During the season, large shipments of imported herring were landed on the North Sea market. These were bought by the local fish curing companies, to be turned into kippers.

On a winter's evening in February 1952, a barrow-lad takes a consignment of fish to a railway fish van. Each van in the train had its destination chalked up on the side.

One of the main reasons that Hull became such a prominent fishing port was its early rail links with the industrial cities of the north of England.

For over a hundred years fish trains took Hull fish to distribution points throughout the country. But in July 1964, British Railways under the Dr. Beeching re-organisation, reduced the number of Hull fish train from 8 to 2 a day. Then in 1965 the rail service was completely withdrawn.

With the departure of the fish trains the dock lost a great part of its character. The sounds of the fish trains being shunted off the dock to various destinations punctuated the working day and life was never the same without them.

By the afternoon the fish market became relatively quiet. The kit scrubbers have washed and stacked the kits ready for the following day. The bobbers have gone home and the only noise would come from the fish filleters, still at work boxing fish.

Having landed her catch at Hull, the *Jegvan Elias Thomsen* is waiting to sail back home to the Faroe Islands. The vessel was once the Hull trawler *Lammermuir* (H105) which was sold to Faroese owners in 1956.

Hovering above the market is the inevitable flock of seagulls, which are on the lookout for scraps of fish that are washed into the dock as the market floor is hosed clean.

93

CHAPTER 9

TRAWLER COMPANY OFFICES AND PREPARATION FOR SEA: DRY SIDE

Once a trawler had landed its catch it was towed over to the ice factory to take on a supply of fresh ice. Chutes directed the flow of ice straight into the trawler's fishroom pounds.

Occasionally trawlers had to queue for their turn under the chute as is the case with this picture taken on 21 February 1957. The trawlers on the left are:- *Arctic Scout* H143 and *Scalby Wyke* H138. In the right-hand corner shore-gangs are loading cans of engine lubricating oil.

The Hull Ice Manufacturing Company was a non-profit making company, run for the benefit of the Hull fishing industry. The company's first factory was opened in 1894.

The Ice factory on the southside of St. Andrew's Dock was equipped with plant that made it the biggest in Europe.

Seven giant compressors provided the refrigeration to produce up to 1300 tons of ice a day should the demand arise. The ice was produced in eight tank rooms from where it was conveyed to four refrigerated store-rooms. On the top floor were housed the five pulversising plants which broke up the blocks of ice into its crushed form.

This view of the interior of the ice factory dates from 1955.

In this photograph taken in 1956, three trawlers are being repaired during their short stay in port.
Early in the morning whilst a trawler was still on the market a meeting would take place between the trawler Skipper,
Mate and Chief Engineer, the shore-gang foreman and also the ship repair company's manager.
This was to discuss any problems encountered during the last trip and any repairs that needed to be done before the trawler returned to sea.
To the left of the picture a shore-gang is being given instructions prior to boarding the *St. Britwin* H124.
Repair workers have already started work on *Loch Seaforth* H293 (centre) and the *Victrix* H428 (right).
Among tradesmen at work on all parts of the ship would be:- welders, blacksmiths, boiler-makers, sheetmetal workers, engineers, carpenters,
electricians, plumbers, shipwrights, painters, riggers and wireless-radar technicians.
Occasionally the repairs would not be completed during the trawler's allotted time in port (48-60hrs).
This would mean the vessel would be delayed from sailing, much to the delight of some of the crew.

This view taken in 1950 shows fishing gear being loaded into a trawler's fo'c's'le or forecastle net store.
Placed in a handy position near to the foredeck
the store contained all the equipment to keep the trawler's fishing gear in good working order.
i.e:- spare trawls, twine, rope, wires, grease, head line floats, bobbins etc.
Also in this era the fo'c's'le was the home of the deck hands. Here they slept and rested in bunks placed around the bulkheads.

In the 1950's trawlers were fitted out with the new aluminium fish room pound shelf boards which replaced the traditional wooden ones.

In this photograph from 1959, the Boyd Line shore staff have formed a "chain gang" to load a consignment of new boards aboard the *Arctic Viking* H452.

The British Road Services lorry has brought the boards from Sheffield, the city famous for steel and alloy products.

This picture of coal teamers at work coaling up the trawler *Lord Ancaster* H583 was taken in 1949.

As well as the coal carried in the bunkers an extra supply was loaded into the rear of the fish room which was connected to the stokehold via a tunnel. The coal in the fish room was used up on the outward journey to the fishing grounds before the trawler started fishing.

Even though the early oil burning trawlers built in 1946 were proving to be a success, not all owners opted for the new technology and new coal-fired trawlers were built for the Hull fleet until 1948.

But during the 1950s the number of coal burning trawlers declined due to a combination of coal burners being converted to fuel oil and older vessels being either sold to other ports or scrapped. From a peak of 122 coal burning trawlers in 1946 by 1959 only 7 remained and the last 4 were laid up for scrapping in 1962.

Hellyer Brothers' trawler *Othello* H581 had the distinction of being the last coal-burning trawler to sail out of Hull. Her demise in 1962 brought another one of the dock's historic activities to an end.

Dock craft played an important part in the fish dock operations. Various types of vessels could be seen at work servicing the trawlers in St. Andrew's Dock.

Moored alongside the *Cape Crozier* H568 in 1963 are an oil barge and the tug *Wilberforce* which were owned by John W. Whitaker of Hull. The other craft waiting to come alongside is one of the fresh water barges.

Another prominent supplier of fuel oil to trawlers was John Harker of Knottingley whose vessels ended in the suffix H, i.e. *Langdale H*. (The company was eventually acquired by Whitakers of Hull).

A number of vessels were registered to work at St. Andrew's Dock. They were:- Hull Trawlers' Supply Company's *Necessity, Vitality* and *Equality*. Marfleet Refining Company (cod liver oil) *Oilco No. 3, Oilco No. 4* and *Oilco No.6*. The Tug Committee ran the fishdock tugs, *Kiero, Triune, Bernie, Dagger* and *Gilder*. These steam tugs were later replaced by modern vessels *Aurora, Triton* and *Zephyr*. Most of these vessels were for some reason named after old-time Hull whalers!

Also to be seen at work in the dock were the dredgers owned by British Transport Docks Board and the diver's boat.

The Hull Fish Meal & Oil Company's factory was situated at the south-west end of the St. Andrew's Dock extension. This early 1960's photograph shows one of the company's fleet of lorries being loaded with bags of fish meal from a conveyor in one of the loading bays.

The head and backbone of processed fish were placed in kits and sent to the factory. Also any unsold fish from a trawler's catch ended up here. Sadly in times of fish gluts this included good quality fresh fish as well.

The Hull factory was the biggest wet fish meal factory in the world, with a daily intake capacity of 1,000 tons, of which 650 tons could be processed.

The pungent aroma coming from the factory would soon have any newcomer's nose twitching but local workers and residents were immune. When the weather conditions were right the smell pervaded the city centre and the whole of west Hull!

The factory continued processing fish offal until 1987, when the former St. Andrew's Dock was turned into a leisure and industrial park, named St. Andrew's Quay.

Decorated for the celebrations of the Coronation of H.M. Queen Elizabeth II on 2 June 1953 are the offices of Hudson Brothers Trawlers Limited.

These premises which were situated on the south side of St. Andrew's Dock, were typical of the buildings trawler owners used, providing all the facilities required to run a trawler fleet.

Among the people working in such an office would be:- Trawler owner, Manager, Engineering Superintendent, cashiers, accountant, secretaries, fish sales staff, ship's husband, ship's runner, shoregang, riggers, shipwrights, tinsmiths and watchmen.

The old established company of Hudson Brothers dates back to 1913 as Hull trawler owners. The company's trawlers were named after CAPES e.g. *Cape Crozier*. The company became part of Ross Group on 5 February 1960.

One of the most famous old Hull trawler companies was the Kingston Steam Trawling Company whose trawlers were named after precious stones.

In this 1950s photograph two trawlermen are looking at the display cabinet which contained an example of a stone of all the ships that were in the company's service at the time.

When the picture was taken the cabinet had the following stones: Agate, Almandine, Amber, Andalusite, Beryl, Diamond, Emerald, Garnet, Jacinth, Jade, Onyx, Pearl, Peridot, Ruby, Sapphire, Sardius, Topaz, Turquoise and Zircon.

Other post-war vessels not represented in the case would be Aquamarine, Chrysoberyl, Chrysolite, Coral, Crystal, Cyanite, Galena and Olivine.

From the mid-1920's the company's trawlers carried the prefix *Kingston*.

In 1966 the company became extinct when all its ships were re-registered in the name of Hellyer Brothers.

CHAPTER 10 : TRANSPORT AND OFF-DOCK PROCESSING

Over the years a large number of fish processing factories were built in the streets near to the St. Andrew's Dock estate. These factories provided a considerable amount of work for the men and women of the local Hessle Road community, working as filleters and fish packers.

Vast amounts of white fish, mainly cod, were required to supply the large factories of the frozen food giants:- Bird's Eye, Ross and Eskimo. White fish is used to make a wide range of convenience foods like fish fingers, fish cakes, cod in parsley sauce etc.

These companies, Bird's Eye especially, bought large amounts of codling on the Hull fish market and offered out the work of cutting the fish for local fish merchants. The main ones who carried out the work were Macfisheries, Harry Markham, Mat Anderson, F. Smales and C. Westlake.

Macfisheries, which was part of the Unilever group, was a large fish processing company owning factories at most major fishing ports. At Hull they had factories in West Dock Street and Gloucester Street. As well as supplying the wet and fried fish trades, the company cut fish for the frozen food industry.

In the relatively comfortable interior of one of Macfisheries factories, filleters are cutting a consignment of codling. This photograph was taken on 3 May 1961.

In this second photograph taken on 3 May 1961 women are weighing and packing Bird's Eye cod fillets in the Macfisheries factory.

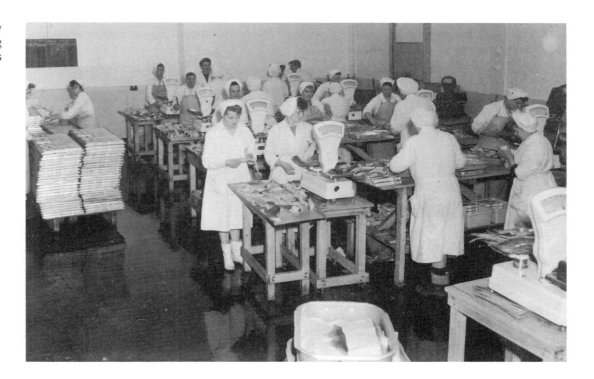

This photograph shows a team of four women "tenterers" working at a tub preparing kippers at the Eskimo factory on 29 November 1957.

At the factory herring were split open and the offal and gills were removed. The herrings were then washed and packed in pickling brine for between 20-30 minutes. With four women working each tub, the herring was pressed onto "boaks" which were strips of wood 3'6" long which were filled with hooks set at an angle. When each boak was full the women would take them to the smoke house. When the smoke house was full fires of oak sawdust and wood shavings would be lit and it was the smoke from this that gave the kippers such an excellent flavour.

In this photograph taken at Cadora's curing premises on 11 November 1954, women packers are checking the quality of smoked cod fillets before packing them into wooden boxes. To the left are two bays full of smoked haddock.

In the preparation of these products codling fillets were placed into vats of coloured brine where they soaked for a while. This gives them the nice yellow colour. They were then hung to dry on a rack prior to being placed in the smoke house.

Haddocks were headed, split down the middle, washed and well cleaned then speated onto steel rods and hung to dry prior to being placed in the smoke house.

Apart from smoked fish Hull also had a big salt fish industry. A number of local companies are still producing cured and salt fish products at Hull.

Cadora Ltd. was one of Hull's fifty fish curing companies, their products distributed throughout Britain.

In this photograph dating from 1954, one of the company's lorrys is being loaded with wooden boxes of smoked fish at the Essex Street factory. The load is made up of Cadora cured cod fillets and D. A. Macrae oak-smoked kippers.

HULL POST-WAR TRAWLER COMPANIES

Associated Fisheries
Boston Deep Sea Fisheries
Boyd Line Ltd.
British United Trawlers
Charleson — Smith Trawlers Ltd.
Eton Fishing Company Ltd.
Thomas Hamling & Company Ltd.
Hellyer Brothers Ltd.
Henriksen & Company Ltd.
Hudson Bros. (Trawlers) Ltd.
Hull Merchants Amalgamated Trawlers
Kingston Steam Trawling Company Ltd.

Loch Fishing Company Ltd.
Lord Line
Marine Steam Fishing Company Ltd.
J. Marr & Son Ltd.
Newington Steam Trawling Company Ltd.
The Ocean Steam Trawling Company Ltd.
F & T Ross Ltd.
Ross Group
St. Andrew's Steam Fishing Company Ltd.
Victoria Fishing Company Ltd.
West Dock Steam Fishing Company Ltd.

Some of the main companies also owned a number of subsidiary companies.

LIST OF HULL FISH MERCHANTS 1949

Adams F. W.	Boyd M. H.	Chester J. W.	Double J. W.
Ainsworth & Son T. W.	Bradley A. W.	Clark A.	Drewery & Wilkinson
Albrow R. C.	Bradshaw A. S.	Clark K. Ltd.	Duggleby Bros. Ltd.
Albrow R. C. Jnr.	Brekkes Limited	Class J. H. & Co. Ltd.	Duggleby C. H.
Allen G. M.	Britton H. (Hull) Ltd.	Clubley H. V.	Dukes A.
Allen S. J.	British Fish Curing Co. Ltd.	Coleman T.	Dukes Bros.
Allenby C.	Brown J. R.	Colley J. N.	Dukes W.
Allenby M.	Brown J. W.	Collier G. & T.	Dunn T. W.
Allenby S. E.	Brown & Marriott	Collins H. W. & Co.	
Astley & Son D.	Brown & Sons	Cook F. Snr.	Eagle A.
	Bull A. B.	Cook F. & Sons Ltd.	Edhouse H. & Son
Bainbridge W.	Bull Bros.	Cooke A.	Edwards S.
Banks R.	Bull H. Snr.	Coupland R. & Co.	Elder J.
Barkworth W. L. (Hull) Ltd.	Burns A. O.	Coward T.	Ellerington S.
Bates J. H.	Butcher A.	Crack S. R.	Ellis T. E.
Batty E. & M.	Butler & Draper	Crimlis F. Ltd.	Emslie W.
Beatham R.		Crockford W. A.	England H. Ltd.
Beattie L. R.	Cadora Limited	Curtis F.	Everett J. Jnr.
Beaumont G.	Camp R. R. Ltd.	C. W. S. Limited	
Bennett T. (Hull) Ltd.	Cash H. S.		Farrel J. H.
Bigley W.	Cawley W.	Dale A. Ltd.	Field H. & Son
Blades G. E.	Cawoods (Fish Curers) Ltd.	D'Arcy C.	Field Jeff Ltd.
Boddy S.	Chapman Bros.	Dent G. H.	Fillets Ltd.
Bogg G. F. & Sons	Chapman H.	Dickinson Bros.	Fish Exports Ltd.
Boyd J. H.	Capron H. & Son	Dishman & Degnan Ltd.	Fletcher G.

Fletcher W.
Forester H.
Foster & Son
Foster S. C.
Fosters Freezers Ltd.
Fox Mrs. Mabel
Fuller J.W.

Gant C.
Garforth A. Ltd.
Gee Mrs. L. A. t/a H. Gee
Gibbins G.
Gibbs Chris & Co.
Gibbs G. & Co.
Gibson Bros.
Gillard E.
Gillard N.
Gillard G. & Sons
Gladstone Bros.
Gladstone T. A.
Gladstone W.
Glanville E.
Glenton G.
Gofton H.
Good C. N.
Green A.

Hall H. G.
Hampshire Birrell & Co. Ltd.
Handley T. E.
Hannath G.
Harley & Co.
Harris J.
Harrison Bros.
Harrison C.
Harrison W.
Hart J. & Son Ltd.
Headspith E. & R.
Heald E. Ltd.
Henery A.
Hewtson C. W. & Son
Hildred R. W.
Hill Bros.
Hill & Son
Hilton & Cusworth Ltd.
Hinks F. G.
Hines Bros.

Hodgson & Brand
Holmes W. H.
Horner T. H. (Successors)
Horsley C. L.
Houghton W.
Howard W.
Howson H.
Humphries G.

Inkson H. G.

Jackson & Barker Ltd.
Jackson Mills Ltd.
Jaysmith Bros.
Johnson A. E. & Son
A. Johnson & Knudtzon Ltd.
Johnson C. B.
Johnson Fred
Jones J. F. & Sons Ltd.
Jordan C. W.
Jordan H. M.
Jordan H. P.
Jordan J.

Kemplay R. L.
Kilvington Mrs. C.
Kilvington S.
Knell H. S. Ltd.

Latus G. W.
Law Bros. Ltd.
Lawson & Ashton Ltd.
Lee & Page Ltd.
Lee S. H. (Fleetwood) Ltd.
Lee & Son (Grimsby) Ltd.
Levine J.
Leyman Jackson & Co.
Lill Alan
Lill Bros.
Litten A.
Lofthouse G. W.
Lowery J. C.
Luke G.
Lumb W.
Lyon R. W. & Co.

Macrae D. A.
McCann Bros.
McGrath Bros. Ltd.
Maggs W. H. & Son
Marris C.
Marris C. H.
Marrows C.
Marshall Bros.
Martin & Read
Mathias S.
Mellonie P.
Milner Antcliffe
Milner & Co.
Milner N.
Monge & Co. Ltd.
Montgomery A.
Moody Bros. Ltd.
Moody H.
Moreland H. J. & Sons
Moss P.
Musgraves (Hull) Ltd.

National Fish Curing Co. Ltd.
Nelson E.
Neptune Products Ltd.
Neve J.
Nichol H.
Nicholson N.
North Seas Products Ltd.
Northern C. Fed. F. F. Ltd.
Norton A.
Norton D. Ltd.
Norton J. E.
Nowell S. Ltd.

Paddison H.
Parker F.
Parson T. C.
Pedersen & Co. Ltd.
Percival H. (Fish Mchts) Ltd.
Percy L. Ltd.
Peterson P. M.
Pettman I. C.
Penton G. & Co.
Phillips Jackson Ltd.
Phipps W. & Son

Pibel S. Ltd.
Pickering, Haldane & Co.
Pickles H. Ltd.
Pocklington K. & Co.
Pollard J. S.
Porter A. E.
Porter Bros. (Fish Mchts) Ltd.
Powell R. E.
Prime Products Ltd.
Procter H. G. & Son
Purdy A. E.

Quality T. (Hull) Ltd.

Read S. & J.
Redfern R.
Redgraves R.
Robins A. & W. Ltd.
Robins H. & Co. Ltd.
Robinson A.
Robinson E. T.
Robinson E. & Son
Robinson J. (Hull) Ltd.
Robinson L. & J.
Ross Group (Hull) Ltd.
Rowbottom G.
Royal Fish Co.
Rutter C. Ltd.

St. Andrew's St. Fishing Co.
Sampson & Sons J.
Selby C.
Selby R. F.
Simons & Moore
Scottish Freshing Co.
Smales F.
Smart J. K.
Smart A.
Smith H.
Smith Rowland Ltd.
Smith Wilson J.
Smart J. H.
Snowden & Son W.
Sproston & Crowther Ltd.
Stanley H. R.
St. Dunstans Fishing Co. Ltd.

Stephenson E. J.
Stephenson F. W.
Stirk Bros. Ltd.
Stirk J.
Stonebanks C. F. Ltd.
Stockman & Bolderson Ltd.
Storr (Fish Mchts) Ltd.
Streets F. E.
Stubbins D. & Son
Swann F.

Taylor J.
Tether G. & Sons Ltd.
Tether John

Thewles B. Ltd.
Thomas W.
Tipple W.
Tomlinson J.

Ubique Fish Supply

Walker A. & G.
Waller H.
Walton G. (Hull) Ltd.
Walton W. A.
Webber G. R.
Webber R.
Welham & Sons

Westlake C. Ltd.
Westmoreland F. A.
Westmoreland J. T.
Westwood J. (Hull) Ltd.
White C.
Warcup H. O.
Wight J.
Wingham G. R.
Wingham G. E.
Wignall A.
Wilkinson Bros.
Wilkinson T. R.
Willey W. B. & Sons Ltd.
Wilson W. R. Ltd.

Witherwick G. T.
Woodger J. & Sons Ltd.
Woodliffe Bros. Ltd.
Woods Fish Supply
Wren & Hines
Wright H. M.

Young W. H.
Younger L.
Youngman H.
Youngman & Sons (Hull) Ltd.

Total names: 316

LIST OF SIDE-FISHING TRAWLERS REGISTERED AT HULL
1946 — 1995

Achroite H81
Admetus H395
Admiral Nelson H183
Alamein 1 H283
Alamein 2 H123
Alexandrite H7
Allan Water H420
Almandine H415
Alvis H52
Andradite H26
Anthony Hope H254
Arab H293
Arctic Adventurer H381
Arctic Avenger H118
Arctic Brigand H52
Arctic Buccaneer H516
Arctic Cavalier H204
Arctic Corsair H320
Arctic Crusader 1 H90
Arctic Crusader 2 H333
Arctic Crusader 3 H74
Arctic Explorer H287
Arctic Galliard H209
Arctic Hunter 1 H17
Arctic Hunter 2 H218
Arctic Invader H360
Arctic Outlaw H216
Arctic Ranger 1 H251
Arctic Ranger 2 H155
Arctic Rebel H219
Arctic Rover H402

Arctic Scout H143
Arctic Trapper 1 H567
Arctic Trapper 2 H425
Arctic Vandal H344
Arctic Viking H452
Arctic Warrior H176
Arnanes H567
Arnold Bennett H259
Auburn Wyke H218
Avola H382
Avondale H165
Avonwater H368
Ayrshire H113

Balthazar H359
Banquo H582
Banyers H255
Bardia H302
Bayella H72
Benella 1 H15
Benella 2 H132
Benghazi H66
Benvolio H22
Bernard Shaw H67
Bizerta H163
Borella H240
Boston Fury H252
Boston Hurricane H568
Boston Meteor H114

Boston Seafire H584
Boston Vampire H94
Boynton Wyke H74
Brimnes 1 H165
Brimnes 2 H558
Brontes H236
Brucella H291
Brunham H89
Brutus H28

Caesar H226
Calydon H253
Cambridgeshire H206
Camilla H193
Cape Adair H119
Cape Aragona H143
Cape Barfleur 1 H161
Cape Barfleur 2 H213
Cape Barracouta H267
Cape Campbell H383
Cape Canaveral H267
Cape Cleveland 1 H355
Cape Cleveland 2 H61
Cape Columbia H118
Cape Comorin H139
Cape Conway H271
Cape Crozier H568
Cape Duner H85

Cape Finisterre H355
Cape Gloucester H395
Cape Kanin H586
Cape Mariato H364
Cape Matapan H238
Cape Melville H150
Cape Nyemetzki H16
Cape Otranto H227
Cape Palliser H354
Cape Pembroke H502
Cape Portland H357
Cape Spartel H79
Cape Tarifa H584
Cape Trafalgar 1 H218
Cape Trafalgar 2 H59
Cape Warwick H272
Capt. Oates H287
Carella H4
a2*Carthusian* H162
Cave H643
Cayton Bay H72
Clevela H201
Cloughstone H374
Colwyn Bay H387
Commander Evans H20
Commander Holbrook H223
Commander Nasmith H385

Conan Doyle H251
Coral Island H567
Cordella H572
Cramond Island H558

D. B. Finn H332
Dalmatia H474
Darthema H214
Davy H213
Dayspring H183
Daystar H542
Derna H84
Dunsby H306
Dunsley Wyke H297
Durga H83

Earl Kitchener H345
Eastcoates H393
Esquimaux H297
Etonian H333
Euclase H384
Evander H272

Fairway H130
Falstaff H107
Faraday H195
Farnella 1 H41
Farnella 2 H399
Forbes H567
Frobisher H502
Fyldea H160

Galvani H88
George Hastings H186
Glenella H333
Goodleigh H134
Goth H211

Hackness H20
Harrovian H16
Hausa H262
Heather Island H565
Hildina H222
Howard 1 H160
Howard 2 H271
Hugh Walpole H336

Ian Fleming H396
Imperialist H2

Iolite H372

James Barrie 1 H460
James Barrie 2 H15
Jennett H465
Josena H207
Joseph Conrad H161
Junella 1 H497
Junella 2 H399

Kelt H193
Kings Grey H402
Kingston Agate H489
Kingston Almandine H104
Kingston Amber 1 H471
Kingston Amber 2 H326
Kingston Andalusite 1 H133
Kingston Andalusite 2 H41
Kingston Aquamarine H520
Kingston Beryl H128
Kingston Chrysoberyl H177
Kingston Chrysolite H205
Kingston Coral H242
Kingston Crystal H281
Kingston Cyanite H237
Kingston Diamond H243
Kingston Emerald 1 H479
Kingston Emerald 2 H49
Kingston Galena H217
Kingston Garnet H106
Kingston Jacinth H198
Kingston Jade H149
Kingston Olivine H209
Kingston Onyx 1 H365
Kingston Onyx 2 H140
Kingston Pearl 1 H542
Kingston Pearl 2 H127
Kingston Peridot 1 H55
Kingston Peridot 2 H591
Kingston Ruby H477
Kingston Sapphire 1 H206
Kingston Sapphire 2 H95
Kingston Sardius H588
Kingston Topaz 1 H352
Kingston Topaz 2 H145
Kingston Turquoise 1 H45
Kingston Turquoise 2 H50

Kingston Zircon H108
Kirkella 1 H155
Kirkella 2 H209

Lady Beryl H151
Lady Elsa H286
Lady Enid H702
Lady Hogarth H479
Lady June H299
Lady Madeleine H243
Lady Olwen H283
Lady Philomena H167
Lady Rosemary H477
Laertes H307
Lammermuir H105
Nancella H290
Larissa H266
Leeds United H172
Loch Alsh H150
Loch Doon H101
Loch Erinoll H323
Loch Fleet H569
Loch Hope H220
Loch Inver 1 H164
Loch Inver 2 H110
Loch Leven 1 H186
Loch Leven 2 H82
Loch Melfort H249
Loch Moidart H481
Loch Monteith H232
Loch Oskaig H431
Loch Seaforth H293
Loch Torridon H165
Loch Tulla H225
Lord Alexander H12
Lord Ancaster 1 H414
Lord Ancaster 2 H583
Lord Ashfield H53
Lord Bann H465
Lord Beatty H112
Lord Cunningham H69
Lord Essendon H312
Lord Foyle H17
Lord Fraser H48
Lord Gort H250
Lord Grey H500

Lord Hawke H39
Lord Hotham H231
Lord Howe H19
Lord Irwin H501
Lord Jellicoe H228
Lord Lloyd H263
Lord Lovat H148
Lord Lovel H506
Lord Lynwood H134
Lord Melchett H1
Lord Middleton H282
Lord Montgomery H401
Lord Mountevans H169
Lord Nuffield H473
Lord Plender H191
Lord Portal 1 H406
Lord Portal 2 H192
Lord Rivers H485
Lord Ross H496
Lord Rowallan H9
Lord Sands H503
Lord St. Vincent H261
Lord Stanhope H199
Lord Tay H286
Lord Tedder H154
Lord Wavell H578
Lord Willoughby H36
Lorella H455
Lorenzo H230
Lucida H403

Macbeth 1 H113
Macbeth 2 H201
Man-O-War H181
Marath H414
Marbella H52
Matabele H217
Maxim H164
Mendip H202
Miletus H75
Milyna H133
Monimia H43
Mount Ard H405
Murella H481

Newby Wyke H111
Newland H653

Norland H266
Norman H289
Norrard H50
Northella 1 H244
Northella 2 H159
Northella 3 H98

Olvina 1 H89
Olvina 2 H139
Onslow H167
Ophelia H576
Orsino H579
Othello H581
Oystermouth Castle H378

Peter Cheyney H195
Peter Scott H103
Pict H162
Portia H24
Primella 1 H103
Primella 2 H98
Prince Charles 1 H85
Prince Charles 2 H249
Prince Charles 3 H77
Prince Philip H32
Princess Anne H268
Princess Elizabeth 1 H86
Princess Elizabeth 2 H135
Princess Elizabeth 3 H238
Princess Royal H183

Quantock H161

Rapier H500
Red Plume H83
Red Sword H80
Reighton Wyke H425
Reptonian H363
Roderigo H135
Rosella H336
Ross Anson GY161
Ross Howe H422
Ross Resolution GY527
Rossallian H164
Rudyard Kipling H141

Saronta H390
Sarpedon H142

Saudanes H565
Scalby Wyke H138
Silanion H577
Sollum H369
Somerset Maugham H329
Southella H303
Spaniard H366
Spurnella H414
St. Achilleus H215
St. Alcuin H125
St. Amandus H247
St. Amant H42
St. Andronicus H241
St. Apollo H592
St. Arcadius H207
St. Attalus H167
St. Bartholomew 1 H216
St. Bartholomew 2 H516
St. Botoloph H188
St. Britwin H124
St. Celestin 1 H192
St. Celestin 2 H233
St. Chad 1 H575
St. Chad 2 H20
St. Christopher 1 H573
St. Christopher 2 H88
St. Crispin 1 H399
St. Crispin 2 H86
St. Dominic H116
St. Elstan H484
St. Gerontius H350
St. Giles H220
St. Hubert 1 H104
St. Hubert 2 H142
St. John H254
St. Kenan H360
St. Keverne H158
St. Leander H19
St. Leger H178
St. Loman 1 H381
St. Loman 2 H156
St. Mark 1 H218
St. Mark 2 H520
St. Mark 3 H152
St. Matthew 1 H264
St. Matthew 2 H201

St. Nectan H411
St. Oswald H335
St. Peter H102
St. Romanus H223
St. Ronan H86
St. Stephen H299
St. Wistan H486
St. Zeno H255
Starella 1 H75
Starella 2 H219
Staxton Wyke H479
Stella Altair H279
Stella Antares H123
Stella Aquila H114
Stella Arcturus H216
Stella Canopus H244
Stella Capella H358
Stella Carina 1 H355
Stella Carina 2 H573
Stella Dorado 1 H202
Stella Dorado 2 H307
Stella Leonis H322
Stella Orion 1 H379
Stella Orion 2 H235
Stella Pegasi 1 H90
Stella Pegasi 2 H414
Stella Polaris 1 H383
Stella Polaris 2 H566
Stella Polaris 3 H575
Stella Procyon 1 H162
Stella Procyon 2 H184
Stella Rigel 1 H14
Stella Rigel 2 H170
Stella Sirius 1 H165
Stella Sirius 2 H163
Stella Sirius 3 H277
Swanella 1 H42
Swanella 2 H141
Swanland H402

Tarchon H141
Tervani H530
Tesla H573
Thorina H318
Thornella 1 H582
Thornella 2 H84

Thornwick Bay H241
Tobruk H14
Tripoli H307
Turcoman H163

Velia H239
Vian H406
Victrix H428

Warwick Deeping H151
Westhawk H474
Westhaze H589
Westheron H465
Westhill H470
Westhope H590
Westella 1 H349
Westella 2 H194
White Flower H577
William Wilberforce H200

Yorick H410
Yorkshire Rose H16

Total names: 432.

HULL REGISTERED STERN TRAWLERS

Afghan H237
Arab H238
Arctic Buccaneer H188
Arctic Corsair H320
Arctic Freebooter H362
Arctic Galliard H195
Arctic Privateer H441
Arctic Raider H440
Arctic Ranger H155

Boston York H3

C. S. Forester H86
Cape Kennedy H353
Cassio H398
Cordella H177
Coriolanus H412

Dane H144

Esquimaux H236

Farnella H135

Gaul H243
Gavina H24
Goth H252

Hammond Innes H180

Invincible H96

Junella 1 H347
Junella 2 H294

Kelt H240
Kirkella H367
Kurd H242

Lady Parkes H397

Lancella H98
Lord Nelson H330

Marbella 1 H384
Marbella 2 H771

Norse H193
Northella 1 H301
Northella 2 H206

Orsino H410
Othello H389

Pict H150
Princess Anne H269

Ross Illustrious H419
Ross Implacable H6
Ross Intrepid H353

St. Benedict H164
St. Finbarr H308
St. Jason H436
St. Jasper H31
St. Jerome H442
Seafridge Osprey H137
Seafridge Petrel H175
Seafridge Skua H138
Sir Fred Parkes H385
Southella 1 H40
Southella 2 H240
Swanella 1 H421
Swanella 2 H1065

Thornella H96
Turcoman H233

Total names: 58